The Haiku Seasons

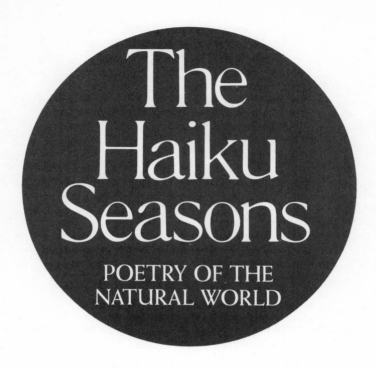

The Haiku Seasons

POETRY OF THE NATURAL WORLD

William J. Higginson

KODANSHA INTERNATIONAL
Tokyo • New York • London

Distributed in the United States by Kodansha America, Inc., 114
Fifth Avenue, New York, N.Y. 10011, and in the United
Kingdom and continental Europe by Kodansha Europe Ltd., 95
Aldwych, London WC2B 4JF. Published by Kodansha
International Ltd., 17-14 Otowa 1-chome, Bunkyo-ku, Tokyo
112-8652, and Kodansha America, Inc.

First edition, 1996
97 98 10 9 8 7 6 5 4 3 2

ISBN 4-7700-1629-8

Library of Congress Cataloging-in-Publication Data
A catalog record for this book is available from the Library of Congress

Dedicated to
Penny Harter
poet and partner
and
Elizabeth Searle Lamb
poet and friend

CONTENTS

LIST OF TABLES

INTRODUCTION TO *THE HAIKU SEASONS*

Submit to nature, return to nature.

Bashō (1644-1694)

... the seasonal theme is one of the elements
which cannot be omitted from the haiku ...

Otsuji Seki (1881-1920)
translated by Kenneth Yasuda

I am quite confident that I have completely liberated myself
from the yoke of the seasonal theme.

Ippekirō Nakatsuka (1887-1946)
translated by Soichi Furuta

Bashō, a master of *haikai no renga* (also called *haikai renga* or
renku, popular linked poems), brought the genre to its peak in
the late seventeenth century. He virtually created what we now
know as "haiku" with the excellence of his independent *hokku*
(originally starting verses for linked poems). He instilled depth
into *haibun* and diary literature by creating powerful prose
poems with haiku, including the incomparable masterpiece
Narrow Roads of the Interior (*Oku no hosomichi*). Bashō's work
also served as a precursor to the *senryū*, short poems on the
humor of human acts and perceptions. Today we may view all of
these as parts of the genre known as *haikai*, a literature written
for a popular audience and involving people from all walks of
life as authors.

Nature, the cycle of the seasons, and love have formed the
core of Japan's poetic perception and expression for centuries.

Traditional poetry anthologies were ordered in sections devoted to related themes; by far the most prominent themes were the four seasons and love. The importance of these led to the primacy of the seasons and a major role for love in linked poetry, both the early courtly *renga* and the later popular *renku*. During the nineteenth and twentieth centuries these themes of renku found expression in the independent verses now known as haiku and senryu. The seasonal themes expanded into a rich specialized vocabulary of "seasonal topics" (*kidai*) and "season words" (*kigo*) which has dominated haiku. The humor of love and other human relationships became the major concern of senryu. Meanwhile renku seemed to disappear.

However, in Japan throughout the twentieth century there have been haiku poets who rejected dogmatic insistence on the season word as haiku's main defining characteristic, senryu poets who included nature beyond human nature in their poems, and at least a few poets quietly meeting to write renku together. Haiku and senryu have now become worldwide poetic genres, and interest in renku has grown substantially both in and outside of Japan. It seems appropriate to examine the relationship of these intimately connected poetries and nature, first in the more than millennium-long Japanese tradition, then in the light of their increasing internationalization.

THE INTERNATIONAL HAIKU SEASONS PROJECT

Since writing *The Haiku Handbook: How to Write, Share, and Teach Haiku*, my wife Penny Harter and I have had many opportunities to visit Japan and learn first-hand the richness of the haikai tradition. We have met and talked and composed poems with dozens of poets in settings as varied as apartments in Tokyo, temple gardens and shrines near Kyoto, boating on the Inland Sea, and mountaintops in Yamagata. And we have come to appreciate the deep connection of haikai with the human and natural world. This travel and practice have led me to study in particular the modern *haikai saijiki* or poetry almanac and its place in the tradition of Japanese poetry and in the lives of poets today.

Since 1987 I have worked on what I call "The Haiku Seasons Project"—an attempt to understand the development of seasonal consciousness in traditional Japanese poetry and its current most striking manifestation, the haikai saijiki, or poetry almanac. In 1990 I wrote a column on the seasonal aspect of haiku for *Frogpond*, the journal of the Haiku Society of America. Many poets sent contributions for "Seasoned Haiku"—responding to my requests for haiku on set traditional topics, or on other topics which they proposed. Accompanying correspondence indicated high interest, and the quality of the poems was comparable to that in the better English-language haiku magazines at the time. The column featured work from poets in Australia, Canada, Mexico, New Zealand, Sweden, and the United States. (I must acknowledge that my column was preceded by similar work in the San Francisco-based Yuki Teikei Haiku Society of the U.S.A. and Canada, beginning as early as 1977.)

Interest in reading and writing haiku has been steadily grow-ing in the Americas, Europe, and elsewhere for some time. For well over a decade Professor Kazuo Satō has directed the International Division of the Museum of Haiku Literature, maintained by the Haiku Poets Association, and edited a column of haiku in English for the *Mainichi Daily News*, a prominent English-language newspaper in Japan. In his work at the museum he has collected haiku books and periodicals in many foreign languages. He and I have been comparing notes on the number of countries involved in haiku for some time, and were delighted in the late 1980s when we found active haiku poets in more than twenty. At the same time, some Japanese haiku clubs have had branches among Japanese expatriates for a number of years, and there are independent Japanese poetry groups in sev-eral countries. I know of Japanese-language haiku and senryu societies in Brazil, Canada, The Netherlands, and the United

States, and I am sure there are many more. The increasing inter-nationalization of haiku was recognized by Japanese haiku poets in 1989, when a group representing the top haiku leadership there formed the Haiku International Association, dedicated to the exchange of haiku and related information between contem-porary Japanese haiku poets and those writing haiku outside of Japan.

In the meantime, I edited *Haiku Southwest*, a newsletter for the Southwestern Region of the Haiku Society of America, in 1993 and 1994. This put me in touch with haiku periodicals around the world at a time when interest in haiku and related poetry was rapidly expanding. New magazines and haiku orga-nizations had started up in Croatia, England, and Romania, join-ing those already active in Canada, Colombia, Belgium, Germany, Holland, Italy, and the United States. As I continued my studies for The Haiku Seasons Project it became evident that not one, but two things were needed. Poets outside of Japan needed more and better information on the seasonal aspect of haiku and related poetry—its roots in the tradition and its mani-festations in the contemporary Japanese poetry scene. And poets both in and outside of Japan needed to see the work produced around the world in the traditional context of a saijiki.

Only a saijiki with poems from many languages and coun-tries would fully legitimize the seasonal aspect of haiku outside Japan, from both a Japanese and a foreign point of view. A majority of poets writing outside of Japan and a majority of Japanese poets both seemed to view the seasonal aspect of foreign haiku as weaker or less important than its dominant role in Japanese haiku. And, it seemed to me, many members of the Japanese haiku community were mesmerized by the seasonal aspect of their poetry to the exclusion of other important matters.

As the quotations at the head of this introduction demon-strate, Japanese opinion on the importance of the seasonal aspect of haiku has been divided. Throughout most of the twentieth century those insisting on the overriding importance of the seasonal aspect have dominated the Japanese haiku scene, mainly by making the saijiki—a compendium of haiku arranged by season—the dominant form of haiku publication. Recently, some new approaches to the saijiki have resulted in the inclusion of nonseasonal haiku. (These are detailed in Chapter 5 of *The Haiku Seasons*.)

Thus, the time is ripe for a multicultural, international look at what haiku and the related poetries of senryu and linked-verse have become during the final decades of the twentieth century. The best lenses for that look seem to be a review of the Japanese tradition that originated these fascinating responses to the universal poetic impulse, and a survey of the best international haiku and related work, organized in the traditional manner in a way that allows the inclusion of both seasonal and nonseasonal poems. To these ends *The Haiku Seasons: Poetry of the Natural World* and its companion volume, *Haiku World: An International Poetry Almanac*, demonstrate the diversity and unity of the various poetries collectively known as haikai—haiku, senryu, and renku—with a broad sampling from all three.

The Japanese haikai or haiku saijiki, common as it may be in Japan, is virtually unknown to the rest of the world. More than just a collection of poems arranged by the seasons, it provides a deep look at Japanese culture and traditions as treated in haiku and related poetry, and serves as a handbook and guide to poets during composition and revision. Most Japanese haiku poets carry a saijiki with them on haiku excursions, or perhaps all the time. It is the one type of haiku book to be found in almost every bookstore in Japan.

The Haiku Seasons shows how the idea of the saijiki developed within the tradition of Japanese poetry, discusses the varieties of haikai poetry and how they relate to the seasons, and explains how a saijiki is organized. Beginning with the *Manyōshū*, *The Haiku Seasons* reviews the entire history of traditional Japanese poetry from a seasonal perspective, with extensive examples in fresh translations. Here are poems from the court tradition, samples of linked poems by masters of renga and renku, and even a portion of a linked poem by Shiki Masaoka and his disciples, never before translated into English.

The Haiku Seasons proposes the creation of an international haikai saijiki, and presents a number of sample entries for such a collection, including poems from many countries. It also tells how poets anywhere, working individually or in groups, can create their own saijiki for enjoyment and as a resource for instruction.

The companion volume, *Haiku World*, is an international collection of 1,000 outstanding contemporary hokku, haiku, and senryu which have not previously appeared in widely distributed publications, all organized not by poet or language or country, but by topic. Its organization closely follows that of the most authoritative Japanese saijiki, but includes many topics not previously recognized in Japanese works and a substantial section of nonseasonal poems. Its 650 or more topic entries help readers understand the phenomena encountered in the poems, which represent many different cultures and environments. An extensive index gives quick access to all of the 3,300 topics and keywords discussed in the text.

Together, *The Haiku Seasons* and *Haiku World* present over 1,150 verses by more than 600 poets writing in 20 languages from 45 countries. This is twice as many languages and countries as were known to have active haikai poets only ten years ago, and three times as many haikai poets as have ever appeared in an anthology in English. A recent estimate suggested that there are over a million haiku poets outside Japan; another claims five million Japanese haiku poets. May the dialogue continue.

A NOTE ON NAMES

In Asian languages names usually appear with the family name first, followed by the given name—the opposite of the way they are presented in most European languages. As the Japanese have become more and more involved with European languages their solutions to the problem of presenting names so that a reader might know which is a family name and which a personal name have included printing family names in all capital letters, as well as putting names in either Eastern or Western order.

The all-capital-letter solution seems to scream out the family name at the reader. Since the given names of haiku, renku, and senryu poets are often more important than the family names, an approach that emphasizes the family name seems unwarranted.

Many Western writers have found it more comfortable to leave names in the Japanese order, probably the way they were first encountered. For scholars this is easy and practical, since their writings often refer exclusively to Japanese names. Meanwhile, Japanese writers and publishers have increasingly used Western languages—there are several fine Japanese newspapers in English, for example. And these Japanese Western-language publishers have almost uniformly moved to putting all names in the same order, the Western order with given name first. Accordingly, all names in *The Haiku Seasons* and *Haiku World* are presented given-name-first, except in the Japanese-language section of the bibliography in this volume.

SPECIAL THANKS

Since publication of *The Haiku Handbook*, a number of Japanese poets and organizations have kindly invited me to join them in various programs. As a result my contact with the current situation of haiku and renku in Japan has expanded considerably. The value of any contribution *The Haiku Seasons* and *Haiku World* may make to international dialogue and understanding derives in large part from the generosity of my many hosts and teachers in Japan, including Shinkū Fukuda, master of the Amanogawa Renku Group, Sado; Kayoko Hashimoto of the Suimei Haiku Group, Urawa; Meiga Higashi, master of the Nekomino Renku Group, Tokyo; Yoshiko Yoshino, president of the International Haiku Salon EPIC, Matsuyama; Yatsuka

Ishihara, master of the Aki Haiku Group, Tokyo; Tohta Kaneko, president of the Modern Haiku Association, Tokyo; Kōko Katō, president of the Kō Haiku Group, Nagoya; Momoko Kuroda, master of the Aoi Haiku Group, Tokyo; Tokihiko Kusama, former chairman of the board of directors of the Haiku Poets Association, Tokyo; The Leisure Development Center, Tokyo; The City of Matsuyama and its Shiki Memorial Museum and its director, Shigeki Wada; Ryūkan Miyoshi, master of the Jigensha Renku Group, Tokyo; Seijo Okamoto, president of the Renku Foundation, Osaka; Kazuo Satō, director of the International Division of the Museum of Haiku Literature, Tokyo; Kin'ichi Sawaki, former president of the Haiku Poets Association, Tokyo; Shun'ichi Shibohta, of Japan Air Lines and the JAL Foundation; Toyokazu Suzuki, senior editor, Fujimi Shōbo and *Haiku Kenkyū*, Tokyo; Ryūsai Takeshita, international secretary of the Modern Haiku Association, Tokyo; Sonō Uchida, president of the Haiku International Association, Tokyo; The City of Ueno, Mie Prefecture, and its Master Bashō Memorial Museum and its head, Shigetaka Yamamoto; Yamagata Prefecture, Gisho Satake, and the organizers of the Bashō Haiku School, 1987; and Michihiro Yanai and the Gichūji-Rakushisha Preservation Association, Kyoto.

Haruo Shirane, director of the Donald Keene Center at Columbia University, kindly read a draft of *The Haiku Seasons* and offered a number of excellent suggestions for improvement.

Elizabeth Searle Lamb, poet, historian of the North American haiku movement, and long-time editor of *Frogpond*, the journal of the Haiku Society of America, read through the manuscripts of both books and kindly corrected a number of errors. San Francisco-based poet Jerry Kilbride, one of the founders of the Haiku Poets of Northern California, did the same.

Meagan Calogeras, Editor at Kodansha International, provided guidance that greatly improved the manuscripts of both books at every stage of development. Much of their coherence and lucidity derives from her efforts. Responsibility for any persisting difficulties in readability remains with the author.

The Witter Bynner Foundation for Poetry funded a translation project at Santa Fe Preparatory School in the latter half of 1994 which in part supported the author during work on both books; my deep gratitude goes to these institutions, and to Foundation Director Steven Schwartz and Headmaster Stephen M. Machen for their generous assistance.

Tadashi and Kris Kondō, founders of the Association for International Renku, Tokyo, have provided me with infallible guidance and unfailing hospitality repeatedly since Tadashi first began instructing me in the ways of linked poetry almost twenty years ago—without which much of my research and delight in haikai would not have been possible.

Paul Hummel, chiropractor, and his staff including Phoebe Hummel, Linda Leonard, Jeff Meyer, and Susan Steffy, kept me going physically when it seemed the body would give up before this project was completed.

Penny Harter, wife and confidante, supported me and this work in more ways than words can tell.

In the coming year I hope to launch an international newsletter devoted to the full range of haikai. For information, please write to me at From Here Press, P. O. Box 2740, Santa Fe, NM 87504.

I hope that *The Haiku Seasons* and *Haiku World* will promote a deeper understanding of haiku and the closely related poetry of hokku, senryu, and linked verse. This understanding may inform and assist in the creative process and the appreciation of its results, but is not intended to limit or hamper that process or appreciation. Do not put history, theory, or organization between yourself and Bashō's pine tree, but use them to help you go out and find the pine tree, so that you may "learn of the pine" directly, and more richly.

William J. Higginson
Santa Fe, November 1995

CHAPTER

1

THE ESSENCE OF HAIKU

People of refinement submit to nature and befriend the
four seasons. . . . Submit to nature, return to nature.

Bashō, 1688

The Japanese *haiku* and its cousin, the satiric *senryū*,
both originated in a style of linked-verse poem called *haikai no
renga*. *Haikai no renga* usually involved a group of poets who met
to compose a single long poem together, a literary amusement
that became popular with the growing middle class during the
Tokugawa era (1603–1868). Bashō (surname Matsuo, 1644–1694)
was an important poet of the time, and his style of *haikai no renga*
eventually became the most popular, continuing right up to the
beginning of the twentieth century. (*Haikai no renga* is frequently
abbreviated *haikai renga*, and sometimes shortened to simply
haikai.)

Throughout the history of *haikai no renga* a tendency grew to
separate the *hokku* or "starting verse" from the longer collabora-
tive poem, or to write hokku singly without going on to make a
linked-verse poem. These hokku often were included in short
prose pieces, or simply selected and published in their own sec-
tions of anthologies of the *haikai* genre. The separate hokku
gradually became completely independent, and by the late nine-
teenth century were called *haiku*; today most people know Bashō
as a haiku poet.

As it separated from the longer linked-verse poem it was originally supposed to begin, haiku retained some characteristics that were essential to a starting verse and omitted others. The starting verse had to be polite to the host of the gathering or the spirit of the place where the poets gathered, which could be a temple or grave site. Since writing haiku solo meant no gathering, this requirement was soon lost. The hokku had to indicate where the poem was composed, usually by naming an object or phenomenon typical of the place; this is not required today, but many haiku still give a strong sense of place. It had to follow certain formal and grammatical rules, which Japanese traditionalists still observe. And most important, it had to express a "seasonal feeling"—to show the season, often right down to the month or even the day, in which it was written.

This last requirement, showing the season, has been the single most important aspect of traditional Japanese hokku and haiku for almost four hundred years. Even the relatively few twentieth-century iconoclasts, who have abandoned formal constraints and refused to think about traditional ways of indicating the seasons, have written many poems including seasonal feelings. (Haiku form does not concern us here, but is discussed in *The Haiku Handbook: How to Write, Share, and Teach Haiku*. See the bibliography.)

Kisetsu, or seasonal feeling, comes easily to those living in Japan. The main Japanese islands span a width of temperate geography comparable to the stretch of North America from Maine to Florida or Oregon to Baja California, of Europe and Africa from northern France to the Sahara, of mainland Asia from Mongolia to Bangladesh, and of Australia and New Zealand from the tip of South Island to Queensland. But until very recently, the weather patterns and climate of Kyoto or Tokyo, both controlled by the warm Japan Current in the Pacific Ocean, have dominated the Japanese perception of the seasons. This has been particularly true in Japanese literature, where common perceptions often become traditions within a generation.

Since the majority of the Japanese people live in or near the area between Tokyo to the northeast and Kyoto and Osaka to the southwest, and the center of Japanese political power and social status has remained in this region since prehistoric times, its climate is the climate of Japanese literature. And the seasons in this area have highly noticeable boundaries. Spring begins while snow is still on the ground, with the delicate, perfumed blossoms of ornamental plum trees. On a February morning Bashō sings:

mume ga ka ni	in the scent of plum
notto hi no deru	suddenly the sun comes out—
yamaji kana	mountain path

Not all spring action takes place in the air, however. Midorijo Abe (1886–1980) with her sharp eye catches something few may have noticed, looking at the ground, where

keichitsu ya	the bug comes out
yōji no gotoku	of hibernation, infant-like
ashi narashi	works its legs

Spring peaks with the massed April luminescence of cherry blossoms, as we look up again with Seimin Horiguchi (b. 1923). He celebrates by

hi o keshite	dousing the light
miru yozakura no	I see the night-time cherries'
ikizukai	breathing

Each of these poems includes a word or phrase traditionally associated with early, middle, or late spring (plum, bug comes out of hibernation, night-time cherry—"blossoms" is understood). Of course, these phrases simply name phenomena common at that time of year in central Japan. It happens that the phenomena are striking enough that people notice them and write haiku about them.

In early times, most Japanese lived very close to nature. The timing of seasonal events was common knowledge. Poets just wrote of what they experienced, and everyone reading their work understood the implied season without thinking too much about it. But it soon became the custom to arrange written poems according to the seasons.

To place poems in seasonal order, one needs criteria for recognizing their seasons. From the earliest times, specific words and phrases began to be noted as carrying seasonal meaning in addition to their normal functions as the names of things, actions, and events. Today the Japanese call these words and phrases "season words" (*kigo*), and have created many books of poems ordered according to a logical arrangement of their season words.

Since season words often name common, everyday things, it is not always necessary to think about season words to include them in a poem. Thus such poets as Santōka Taneda (1882–1940), Seisensui Ogiwara (1884–1976), Hōsai Ozaki (1885–1926), and Ippekirō Nakatsuka (1887–1946), the four most prominent maverick haiku poets of the first half of the twentieth century, are easy to include in seasonal haiku collections, for they name plants, animals, events, and other natural things that happen to be seasonal phenomena in many of their formally irregular poems.

For example, here are two possible "summer" haiku:

poroporo shitataru ase ga   the amply dribbling sweat
masshiro no hako ni   onto the pure white boxes

Santōka

kuraki yo no ko o   on the dark-night sea
oyogu fushi mogusa   swim father and son—seaweed
sukoshi nagare ki   comes flowing a little

Ippekirō

Santōka's poem is from a series on carrying white boxes containing the remains of dead soldiers, after cremation. "Sweat" and "swimming" are traditional season words relating to summer. One suspects that the swim was in summer, but the war scene may have produced its sweat from the heat of the crematorium, indoors or out, any time of year. Still, knowing that Santōka and Ippekirō probably did not care about the seasonal aspects when they wrote these does not mean we distort their meanings if we visualize them in summer.

The following haiku give no clue as to season:

ipponbashi o	over the one-log bridge
kodomo ga kuru	a child comes
inu ga kuru asa	a dog comes: morning

Seisensui

umi ga sukoshi mieru	the sea a little visible
chiisai mado hitotsu motsu	I carry a small window

Hōsai

It would take much rationalization to place these poems in a seasonal context without information from outside the poems themselves.

Santōka, Seisensui, Hōsai, and Ippekirō declined to pay much attention to the seasonal basis of traditional haiku; others who were quite devoted to including seasonal references in their poems did, occasionally, write haiku without season words. One important example is Shiki Masaoka (1867–1902), who despite his brief, disease-ridden life fomented revolutions in three different genres of Japanese literature. He is best remembered for his haiku, and for promoting a theory of painting, "drawing from life" (*shasei*), as the basis for literary art. This theory—usually translated as "drawing from nature"—resulted in a relatively

23

straightforward kind of writing, exemplified in such haiku as Shiki's:

karinokosu	on the cut-over
susuki no kabu no	pampas grass stalks
yuki takashi	the snow's tall

While Shiki wrote thousands of seasonal poems, a few hundred of his haiku cannot be placed by season, according to Japanese authorities. For example:

ten to chi no	heaven and earth's
saebashira ya	supporting column ...
fuji no yama	Mount Fuji

yamamoto no	peeping into sight
koya o nozokeba	at the mountain's foot a hut—
sōzu kana	ah, good water

One might say that the tone of "heaven and earth's . . . Mount Fuji" is congratulatory, and suggest that the poem be classified in the New Year. *Sōzu* ("satisfying water") resembles *shimizu* ("clear water"), a summer season word, so "peeping into sight" might with reason be included in summer. But neither of these poems contains a recognized *kigo*, so they are classified as *zō*—miscellaneous—in the comprehensive collection *Shiki's Haiku Arranged by Season Word* (*Kigo-betsu shiki kushū*), published by the Shiki Museum in his hometown, the City of Matsuyama.

This word *zō*, in haikai contexts, usually means the same thing as "seasonless" (*muki*), and designates verses without specific seasonal reference. Shiki is not the only traditionalist to write haiku fitting this category. Among the thousand or so hokku written by Bashō himself, scholars number about ten as *zō*, including these two:

yo ni furu mo	passing through the world
sara ni sōgi no	indeed this is just
yadori kana	Sōgi's rain shelter

asa yosa o	morning and evening
tare matsushima zo	someone waits at Matsushima!
katagokoro	one-sided love

The first of these is based on a verse by Sōgi (1421–1502), a master of linked-verse composition. Bashō simply replaced "rain shower" (*shigure*) with Sōgi's name; the original runs:

yo ni furu mo	passing through the world
sara ni shigure no	indeed this is just
yadori kana	a shelter from the shower

These verses on shelter note the temporary aspect of that shelter, and of our "passing through the world". Since *shigure* is a winter season word—there are other words for showers in other seasons—Bashō deleted the seasonal reference by replacing it with the earlier poet's name. But most of the people he wrote with and for would have recalled Sōgi's original, and thus probably felt the poem to belong to winter, even though technically it has no place in the seasonal system.

The poem on Matsushima, a group of islands comprising one of the greatest scenic views in all Japan, gives no hint of a season, however. It was published in Bashō's day in the brief *zō* section of a seasonal collection. In the seventeenth century it was not unusual for poets to make seasonless independent hokku, but such poems were generally thought to be of little worth. Few were published, though some provision was made occasionally. By the twentieth century things had changed.

Since the 1920s a small but significant number of Japanese haiku poets have ignored season words, or at least written many poems without them. In the meantime, the seasonally organized haiku collection became the mainstay of haiku publishing. As a result of polarization between haiku traditionalists and poets of seasonless haiku, most modern editors of "haiku almanacs" (*haiku saijiki*) have simply ignored poems which did not fit into their seasonally organized books. At the same time, these saijiki have become the most important type of book on haiku, serving both as substantial anthologies to be read for pleasure and as guides for those who wish to compose haiku of their own. A Japanese bookstore, however small, is very likely to have at least one book on haiku—a saijiki edited by a prominent haiku master or scholar.

To summarize the situation: Haiku without season words exist. Modern saijiki have usually included only haiku with season words.

In the last few years, efforts have been made to produce new kinds of haiku collections, based on "images" or "key-words" instead of season words. In the meantime, some masters are now including a *zō* section of haiku without seasons in their saijiki. These developments and the construction and use of a saijiki are discussed further in Chapters 5 and 6. The point here is, if there are haiku without seasons, and indeed there are, what then is truly essential to haiku?

Without becoming embroiled in the antagonistic debates between warring camps of Japanese haiku poets, the two scholars of Japanese haiku who introduced these short poems to a broad audience of English-speaking readers, R. H. Blyth and Harold G. Henderson, each have described haiku for those readers. From among their many comments, I offer these two, which seem to be their most succinct statements on the subject, and which bear directly on our question:

> A haiku is the expression of a moment of vision into the nature of the world, the world of nature.

> [A haiku is] a record of a moment of emotion in which human nature is somehow linked to all nature.

The first of these appears near the beginning of Blyth's thirty-six-page essay on the differences between haiku and senryu in his 1949 book *Senryu: Japanese Satirical Verses*. (On senryu, see Chapter 4.) Since Blyth published this book and the first of his four-volume work *Haiku* that same year, it seems safe to assume that he gave this statement considerable attention.

The second leads off a discussion of technique for those who wish to write haiku in English, in Henderson's pamphlet *Haiku in English*, first published in 1965. In 1968 Henderson and others founded the Haiku Society of America in New York City, and Henderson headed a definitions committee for the society, which came up with a result very close to this as the first sentence of its definition.

The resemblances between the two statements above are striking. Of course, Henderson knew Blyth and his books. They had met and worked together in Japan years earlier on other matters. But I believe that the similarities in the two statements result from the fact that both men knew a great deal about Japanese haiku. They came at it from somewhat different perspectives; Blyth was a British professor of English literature in Japan (he eventually became tutor to the present Emperor, then Crown Prince) with training in Zen Buddhism, and Henderson was a professor of Japanese studies at Columbia University, specializing in Japanese art.

The two men hardly translated in the same way. Here is one of Bashō's poems in their versions:

The autumn full moon:	Harvest moon:
All night long	around the pond I wander
I paced round the lake.	and the night is gone.

The first is from Blyth's *Haiku*, vol. I (1949), the second from Henderson's *An Introduction to Haiku* (1958). These poem translations are more different from one another than the definitions quoted earlier.

Both men went on to say much more about haiku, mentioning this or that formal or technical aspect, something else about content, origins, and so on. But in attempting to grasp the essence of haiku, they agreed: A haiku is the expression (or record) of a moment in which something happened involving the author's perception of nature. There is a connection, a link, between the human and the other. In Bashō's poem we see the brightness of the moon in the way he kept walking around that pool of water.

There are many different kinds of haiku in the Japanese tradition. Some say Bashō's special genius as a teacher was in helping his disciples become more fully themselves, rather than imposing his vision on them. And their poems are quite different from his, and from one another's. Similarly, during the last half-century the Japanese haiku has been adopted and adapted by many poets around the world, all writing in their own languages.

During the early part of the twentieth century some major Western poets made attempts at grasping one or another aspect of haiku. One thinks of the Americans Ezra Pound and Amy Lowell, the Ecuadorian Jorge Carrera Andrade, the French surrealist Paul Éluard, the Greek George Seferis, the Mexican José Juan Tablada. Yet none of these poets, with the exception of Tablada, penetrated deeply into haiku or made it a cornerstone of their work. Now we read their attempts as artifacts, literary history, more than as literature. In haiku they found techniques and ideals which for the most part they went on and applied to other, longer poems.

However, as a result of the work of the Beat poets and the presentation of Japanese haiku in accessible books by Blyth and Henderson—which all began three or four decades ago here and there in North America and Europe—haiku developed and spread throughout the world, and today we are the beneficiaries of the work of those pioneers. Today people write haiku in Arabic, Catalan, Chinese, Croatian, Danish, Dutch, English, French, German, Italian, Portuguese, Romanian, Russian, Spanish, Swedish, and other languages. Many of these haiku poets have devised "rules" that work for them, and which they in some cases teach to others. But wherever something really akin to haiku has emerged, we judge the results by intuitively seeking the essence of haiku in the poems.

The inclusion or not of a season word has to do with rules, not with essences, or so it seems to a number of haiku poets, both in and outside of Japan. If a poet writes a brief poem that captures a moment, that dives deep into the mystery of the simplest things and actions presented to us every day, chances are we will see nature's face within it, that it will be a haiku.

The chances are also pretty good that such a poet will, intentionally or not, include open clues as to the time of year the event recorded in the poem takes place. For haiku traditionalists season words make the best clues. While the majority of poets writing haiku in languages other than Japanese have not worried much about season words but have generally tried to capture the natural life around them, many of their poems do reflect the seasons in much the same way as traditional Japanese haiku. But few have tried to organize their poems into a traditional saijiki. This book presents the background of the saijiki—its history, organization, and use—with examples from both within and outside of the Japanese tradition. The companion volume, *Haiku World: An International Poetry Almanac*, demonstrates that haiku (and related poems) by poets worldwide can be organized and appreciated in the context of a saijiki.

Since the earliest poetry collections in Japan, people have gathered poems to show off the achievements of their literature and their times, and for the pleasure of readers—and also to instruct. The saijiki is perhaps the ultimate realization of these three goals. It developed out of the desire to collect haiku poems in a way that would help and encourage beginning writers of haiku. As the Japanese themselves have long realized, the main audience for haiku is other haiku poets, or those who might like to take up writing haiku. So the same type of book serves to record poetic accomplishment, entertain aficionados, and teach those new to the genre what it is all about.

In addition to the usual seasonal phenomena, *Haiku World* includes a substantial section of apparently seasonless poems, so that the full range of haiku and senryu, as actually written in Japan and around the world, will be reflected. Hokku (starting verses) from linked-verse poems are also included, to better represent the whole genre called *haikai*. These developments are not so revolutionary as they sound, as the following chapters explain.

CHAPTER

2

THE SEASONS IN OLDER JAPANESE POETRY

From olden times generations of emperors, on a morning of
spring blossoms or a moonlit evening in autumn, summoned
attendants to compose poems appropriate to the occasion.

Ki no Tsurayuki, c. 905

In this first important critical statement on Japanese poetry,
"a morning of spring blossoms" or "a moonlit evening in autumn"
are cited as occasions to compose a poem. Further on in his
introduction to the *Kokinshū* (Ancient and Modern Collection),
Tsurayuki notes that the emperor asked for the poems in
the anthology to be selected in order, starting with wearing
plum blossoms (spring), the sound of the *hototogisu* (a bird of
the cuckoo family with a pleasing song—summer), picking
autumn leaves, and snow viewing (winter). These were to be fol-
lowed by congratulatory poems, love poems, religious poems,
and other "miscellaneous poems which have no spring, summer,
autumn, or winter" and therefore would not be appropriate in
the seasonal sections.

In fact, the emperor's request well describes the organization
of the eleven hundred or so poems in the *Kokinshū*. The poems
are carefully organized into numbered scrolls (usually called
"books" today). The first half contains books of poems on spring,

summer, autumn, and winter, then moves on to other things; the second half leads off with five books on love, followed by miscellaneous poems not otherwise classifiable. These poems are all in the classical thirty-one-sound form called "short poem" (*tanka*) today.

The *Kokinshū* was the first of more than twenty anthologies compiled by imperial command over the next five hundred years, and it set the pattern the others were to follow. But a century and a half before the *Kokinshū*, the first anthology of native Japanese poetry paid great heed to nature and the seasons in both content and organization. A more complex work, the *Manyōshū* includes more than four times as many poems as the *Kokinshū*, in twenty books. Many books have poems on specific topics, or from particular geographical areas or groups of people. And several have substantial sections devoted to the seasons, love, or other topics, including "miscellaneous" poems. These early classifications seem to indicate that even in preliterate Japan, the seasons came to be viewed as important subject matter, and as basic to principles of organization that would guide later compilers of all types of native poetry.

While the poetry of the *Kokinshū* demonstrates the extremely refined sensibility of the stable, aristocratic courtiers of Kyoto, the earlier *Manyōshū* often suggests the fresh breezes of the countryside. Periodically, Japanese poets and critics have recommended a return to the immediacy of Manyō poems like the following, all from the seasonal sections of Book Eight:

iwa-bashiru	Over the rapids
tarumi no ue no	of rock-raging Tarumi
sawarabi no	the fern sprouts
moeizuru haru ni	burst out—it seems now
narunikeru kamo	spring has fully arrived!

Prince Shiki (d. 716)

Some see "Tarumi" as meaning "cascade"; I have taken it as a place name; "rock-raging" (*iwa-bashiru*) seems to be a pillow

word. "Pillow words" (*makura kotoba*) served as meaning ampli-
fiers, much like the "wine-dark" sea in Homer.

natsu no nu no	In a summer meadow
shigemi ni sakeru	blossoming in a thicket
himeyuri no	the red starlily:
shiraenu no koi wa	this unrevealed love
kurushiki mono zo	such a painful thing!

Lady Ōtomo of Sakanoe (fl. 750s)

Himeyuri literally means "maiden-lily"; it is more prone to
shade, has a smaller, more erect blossom and a deeper color than,
say, the tiger lily.

sahogawa no	Saho River's
mizu wo sekiagete	waters dammed up—
ueshi ta wo	the planted paddy's
karu wasaii wa	first rice harvest
hitori narubeshi	better be mine alone.

A Nun and Ōtomo no Yakamochi (716–85?)

When an anonymous nun composed the first three lines, one
of the most prominent poets of the era completed the poem.
Scholars believe Yakamochi was the main compiler of the
Manyōshū, in which this is the only collaboration in tanka form,
called *tan renga* (short linked poem). Toward the end of the
growing season farmers held water back from the paddies; when
the fields dried out they cut the ripened rice. Apparently
Yakamochi thought the first fruits of the field a delicacy worth
flirting over.

waga seko to	Were my man
futari mimaseba	and I to view it together
ikubaku ka	how very much

33

> *kono furu yuki no*   this falling snow
> *ureshikaramashi*   would pleasure me.

Empress Kōmyō (701–60)

These four poems demonstrate the way the lives of the Japanese people, even aristocrats well insulated from the harsher realities, have been intertwined with nature both in fact and in literature. Whether as an object for rejoicing, a conscious metaphor, a thinly veiled invitation, or an occasion for noticing the pain of separation, the natural world has permeated Japanese poetry from the earliest times. And though three of the poems clearly have direct amorous meanings or at least overtones, all of them were classified by season in the *Manyōshū*. Whether their seasons are named or not, each obviously fits only a particular time of year.

Explicitly seasonal groupings make up only a modest percentage of the *Manyōshū*, which opens with a section titled "Miscellaneous Poems" (*zōka*). Many of the first pieces, "long poems" (*nagauta* or *chōka*) in praise of the land of Yamato, mention a variety of natural phenomena which may or may not have seasonal associations. Several books of the *Manyōshū* are named for and include poems from geographical regions or social groups, rather than being based on content.

By the time of the *Kokinshū* (more formally known as the *Kokin Wakashū*), compiled around 900 C.E., things had changed. The following table, simplified from Helen Craig McCullough's study *Brocade by Night: 'Kokin Wakashū' and the Court Style in Japanese Classical Poetry*, shows the arrangement of the numbered books or scrolls of the *Kokinshū*, and the numbers of poems in each book.

BOOKS OF THE *KOKINSHŪ*

BOOK NUMBER AND TITLE	POEMS	BOOK NUMBER AND TITLE	POEMS
1 Spring, vol. 1	68	11 Love, vol. 1	83
2 Spring, vol. 2	66	12 Love, vol. 2	64
3 Summer	34	13 Love, vol. 3	61
4 Autumn, vol. 1	80	14 Love, vol. 4	70
5 Autumn, vol. 2	65	15 Love, vol. 5	82
6 Winter	29	16 Laments	34
7 Felicitations	22	17 Miscellaneous, 1	70
8 Parting	41	18 Miscellaneous, 2	68
9 Travel	16	19 Misc. Forms	68
10 Names of Things	47	20 Folk Songs	32

The books of the *Kokinshū* divide into two halves, of 468 and 632 poems, respectively. The first half begins with poems on the seasons, and these make up about three-quarters of the first half. The second half starts with love, and these poems account for over half of that part. There are a few more poems in the love books than in the seasonal books, and together the seasonal and love books include over 700 of the 1,100 poems in the collection.

Many of the poems in the *Kokinshū*'s love books also have seasonal references but are classified under love since they deal mainly with relationships between lovers, hoped-for or real. For example, the first of the following poems, from the first autumn volume, is apparently so placed because it deals mainly with a phenomenon especially noticed in autumn and the poet's feelings aroused by it, while the second, from the fifth love book, centers on the same image, but uses it to express the emotions involved in a human relationship.

> *tsuki mireba*　　　　Seeing the moon
> *chiji ni mono koso*　　I have these sorrows
> *kanashikere*　　　　　by the thousands

> *waga mi hitotsu no*   though not for me alone
> *aki ni wa aranedo*   does the autumn come.

Ōe no Chisato (fl. 890)

> *ai ni aite*   A fitting grief
> *mono omou koro no*   as I think about things—
> *waga sode ni*   on my sleeve
> *yadoru tsuki sae*   lodges even the moon
> *nururu kao naru*   with its dampened face.

Lady Ise (fl. 890–930)

The opening line of the second poem repeats a pun on the word for "love" (*ai*), which probably accounts for the poem's placement among the love poems. Also, in classical poetry wet sleeves are almost invariably a metaphor for crying, usually in grief over a lover's absence. But the similarity of the two pieces demonstrates the subtlety of the judgements Tsurayuki and his cohorts made when they put these poems in their respective places.

Note that while the earlier *Manyōshū* includes many love poems in seasonal sections, in the *Kokinshū* they are relatively uncommon in the seasonal books. In part this may be because the *Manyōshū* is more loosely organized, with each untitled book subdivided into sections by content or source. For the *Kokinshū*, a conscious decision to title and arrange whole books according to content appears to have governed the organization.

Many poems in the other sections of the *Kokinshū* also have seasonal elements. But the poems in the seasonal books are almost all explicitly about the seasons and associated natural phenomena, while those in the other sections tend to use natural phenomena as metaphors for activities and emotions surrounding the human situations of travel, parting, death, and so on.

> *shio no yama*   The plovers living
> *sashide no iso ni*   on the strands of Sashide
> *sumu chidori*   by Shio Mountain

kimi ga miyo o ba   cry out: "May our Lord reign
yachiyo to zo naku   for eight thousand years!"

Anonymous

For example, in this poem near the beginning of Book Seven, Felicitations, the cries of plovers—a traditional winter image— become congratulatory. They say plovers cry "chiyo"—a homonym for *chiyo*, "a thousand years"—here amplified to "eight thousand years"—*yachiyo*. In a different context the image of plovers crying might have only its seasonal association, but in a congratulatory poem the seasonal aspects, while still present, shift to the background as other symbolic values come to the fore. Since this is only the third poem immediately following the winter book, with no images explicitly from other seasons inter- vening, it helps create a sense of transition. From nature as the subject of the poem, we have moved to nature speaking for the poet.

These two aspects of nature, as subject, and as a means to metaphorical speech, occur in all the great lyric poetries of the world, and might almost be said to define what "lyric poetry" is. They continue to pervade Japanese court poetry through the twenty later imperial anthologies, including the great *Shinkokinshū* (New Ancient and Modern Collection), compiled at the beginning of the thirteenth century. And the compilers of these anthologies followed the same organizing principles set in the *Kokinshū* three hundred years earlier. Here is a *Shinkokinshū* poem from early in Book One, Spring, its author's most famous piece:

miwataseba   As I look out
yamamoto kasumu   the foothills are hazy
minasegawa   at Minase River—
yūbe wa aki to   what made me think
nani omoikemu   "for evenings, it's autumn"?

Ex-Emperor Gotoba (1180–1239)
Gotoba-In (as the name and title read in Japanese) knows that

his readers will be familiar with the way things grow "hazy" (*kasumu*) in spring. So he does not have to tell them that this poem takes place in spring. Japanese aesthetics had long found spring dawns and autumn evenings the most attractive times of day in their respective seasons. But Gotoba looked out from his home at Minase, saw the hazy spring evening, and was so moved by its beauty that he challenged his previous assumption, which was based on the accepted view.

Gotoba commanded the compilation of the *Shinkokinshū* and had much to do with selecting its contents. Despite the implied criticism of convention in the poem above, he was a conservative in an age of political and aesthetic transition.

Princess Shikishi, (Japanese title *naishinnō*, d. 1201; also called Shokushi) was the most prominently featured woman in the *Shinkokinshū*, fifth most prominent overall among the almost four hundred poets included, and this poem helps us see why:

akatsuki no	Daybreak's
yūtsukedori zo	chanticleer!
aware naru	So moving
nagaki neburi o	amid pillow-thoughts
omou makura ni	of "the long sleep" . . .

Princess Shikishi

She has spent a sleepless night alone, contemplating the "long sleep" (*nagaki neburi*), a Buddhist term for this deluded wakefulness we call life. The rooster's crow, normally "lighting the night" and thus warning lovers that night is almost over and they must part, here promises a joyous dawn—the clarity of enlightenment. Extremely compressed, the poem consists of words chosen and placed with great care. Perhaps because the cock-crow is normally found in love poems and has no special seasonal associations, and this tanka is clearly not about love, we find it among the miscellaneous poems of Book Eighteen of the *Shinkokinshū*.

In the poems by Gotoba and Shikishi we see the two poles:

nature as a subject in itself, and natural events used almost allegorically to express ideas.

Buddhist ideas were not restricted to the books of miscellaneous poems (*zō no uta*); this example is from one of the autumn books:

kokoro naki	Even heartless
mi ni mo aware wa	a body would know
shirarekeri	how touching—
shigi tatsu sawa no	a marsh where snipe fly up
aki no yūgure	on an autumn evening.

Priest Saigyō (1118–1190)

Here we see the startling glimpses of the erratic, zig-zag flight of a snipe or snipes rising from the marsh where they have been feeding, and the sweetly melancholy response even of one who has tried to extinguish all desires, all passions. For all his deep religion, here in perhaps Saigyō's most famous poem we see his attachment to the experiences of this world.

Saigyō was the greatest poet of the age, and the *Shinkokinshū* contains almost a hundred of his poems. Nature does not figure in all of them. For example, from Book Eighteen, Miscellaneous:

toshitsuki o	Why does my body
ika de waga mi ni	for months and years
okurikemu	still remain
kinō no hito mo	in this world? People here
kyō wa naki yo ni	just yesterday, gone today.

But this poem is rather atypical. Most of the poems in the "miscellaneous" books do contain natural imagery, like that in the previous poem by Princess Shikishi.

That great novel with almost 800 poems, *The Tale of Genji*, also depends for much of its emotional force on the intimate interrelationships of natural phenomena and human events.

Murasaki Shikibu (late 10th, early 11th c.) underlined the importance of the seasons by having her hero build a palatial residence
with four quarters, each with its own garden—one for each season, and for each of the principal women in Genji's life in these,
his later years. A substantial passage deals with the design and
planting of the four gardens, which correspond to the seasons
most dominant in Genji's relationships with the four ladies.
They also parallel their residents' personalities. Years later, after
the heroine—the lady of the spring quarter—dies, spring seems
to have gone out of Genji's life. In the last chapter in which he
appears, when a visitor comes Genji writes:

waga yado wa	At my house
hana motehayasu	there is no one
hito mo nashi	to admire blossoms . . .
nani ni ka haru no	For what has spring
tazunekitsuran	come looking here?

Genji contemplates his own end later in the same chapter; in
his last poem he muses:

mono omou to	As I think on things
suguru tsukihi mo	the passing days and months
shiranu ma ni	go unnoticed:
toshi mo waga yo mo	will the year and my life
kyō ya tsukinuru	both reach their end today?

For Genji, a man of great aesthetic and human sensitivity,
failure to notice the passage of days and months—of the seasons—means death.

3

LINKED VERSE AND THE SEASONS

The essence of linked verse lies in making everyday
things look fresh.

Nijō Yoshimoto (1320–88)
translated by Makoto Ueda

Yoshimoto compiled the first widely recognized anthology
of "linked poetry" (renga), the Tsukubashū of 1346, and was the
first to write extensively on this collaborative art that is as much a
refined game as it is literature. But more than a hundred years
earlier, Fujiwara no Teika (1162–1241), a member of the group
that selected poems for the Shinkokinshū and the era's leading
tanka poet, seems to have shifted his interest to the new type of
poetry.

Renga was considered a game; some say it began as a relax-
ation after the tension of a poem contest (uta-awase). The earliest
type is the "short linked poem" (tan renga), a few of which appear
in early collections. (One is quoted on page 33.) Renga may even
be related to the dialogue poems recorded in Japan's earliest his-
tories. Certainly the custom of an author composing hundred-
poem sequences of tanka (hyakushu-uta) with varied textures and
images, which grew prominent in the century before the Shin-
kokinshū, helped to establish the ideals of renga.

Originally just an amusement, renga took on the mantle of
serious poetry, adopting and adapting many of the most stringent

rules of courtly tanka and adding rules of its own. Serious renga, for example, were often offered to the gods or to the spirits of the past. The most famous renga ever written, "Three Poets at Minase" (*Minase sangin hyakuin*), was composed in 1488 at the site of Ex-Emperor Gotoba's villa by the greatest master of the genre, Sōgi (1421–1502), and his two leading disciples, Shōhaku (1443–1527) and Sōchō (1448–1532). As this opening stanza, or "starting verse" (*hokku*) makes clear, it was written in memory of the creator of the *Shinkokinshū*. Note how Sōgi's verse echoes Gotoba's poem on spring haze. (See the poem by Gotoba on page 37.)

yuki nagara	Even as it snows
yamamoto kasumu	the foothills are hazy
yūbe kana	this evening

COMMENTARY on Three Poets at Yuyama

"Three poets at Yuyama" (*Yuyama Sangin Hyakuin*) is a hundred-stanza renga in the court style. The first eight stanzas were written on the first page, and a bit more formal in style than the rest. The following comments note each stanza's season or other topic (with the particular word or phrase that indicates the season in parentheses), the connections between stanzas ("links"), and known allusions.

Season: Winter (snow). The immediate surroundings are suggested, with the time of year—as required in the starting verse. Allusion to a tanka by Ōe no Masafusa: "The leaves have fallen/ From the boulder-fenced trees/ In the deep hills./ Over the decaying leaves/ The snow piles up." (tr. Carter)

What follows are the opening stanzas of another renga by Sōgi, Shōhaku, and Sōchō, "Three Poets at Yuyama" (*Yuyama sangin hyakuin*), composed in 1491 at a hot-spring spa. This was a less formal setting, and the poets were more experienced in working together. For connoisseurs, this poem represents the highest attainment in the art of renga. Commentary on the facing pages points out the important features of the stanzas and the links (*tsukeai*) between them, but does not deal with all the complex rules that are being observed. Note, in this and the following examples, how certain words in many of the stanzas indicate a season. My discussion owes a great deal to Steven D. Carter's article "Three Poets at Yuyama: Sōgi and *Yuyama Sangin Hyakuin*, 1491" which appeared in *Monumenta Nipponica*, 1978.

RENGA: THREE POETS AT YUYAMA
(excerpt, stanzas 1–10)

usuyuki ni	Under thin snow
konoha irokoki	the leaves make colorful
yamaji kana	this mountain path
	Shōhaku

Season: Winter, named. Pampas grass, normally an autumnal image, stands out against the rock. Links: Naming the season avoids jumping to autumn, but the suggestion of autumn accords with that in the opening stanza. Word-links: The character for "pampas grass" occurs in the compound for "thin snow"; "rock" also occurs in Masafusa's poem alluded to in the first stanza. Allusion to anonymous *Kokinshū* tanka: "From now on/ may it fall unceasing/ to burden/ my home's pampas grass,/ the flurrying white snow", links snow and pampas grass.

Season: Early Autumn (pine cricket). Links: Realizes the earlier suggestion of autumn. Word-links: "Cricket" and "pampas grass"; "home" and "home" in the anonymous poem alluded to in previous verse.

Season: Autumn (autumn wind). Link: Shifting time of day. Word-link: "Cricket" and "autumn". Allusion to tanka by Fujiwara no Tomoie: "The fall wind blows/ Through my single-spread sleeve/ As the night grows late./ It edges closer to coming out:/ The moon of the mountain rim." (tr. Carter)

Season: Autumn (moon). Word-links: "Moon" and "night"; "cold dew" and "night"; "moon" and "moon of mountain rim" in Tomoie's poem previously alluded to.

Season: None. Topic: Travel (what direction). Word-links: "Field" and "dew"; "have been turning" and "has changed". (Note: The season itself is the "topic" of a seasonal verse.)

Season: None. Topic: Travel (travelers' sky). Link: Needing and getting directions. Word-links: "Travel" and "direction"; "conversation" and "has been turning".

iwamoto susuki
fuyu ya nao min

pampas grass at the rock's base
look at it in winter!

Sōchō

matsumushi ni
sasowaresomeshi
yado idete

by the pine cricket
early I was lured into
leaving my home

Sōgi

sayo fukekeri na
sode no akikaze

so, night has deepened
autumn wind in the sleeves

Shōhaku

tsuyu samushi
tsuki mo hikari ya
kawaruran

the dew is cold
even the light of the moon
has changed

Sōchō

omoi mo narenu
nobe no yukusue

thoughts have been turning—
what direction in the field?

Sōgi

katarau mo
hakana no tomo ya
tabi no sora

even talking
a fleeting friendship . . .
travelers' sky

Shōhaku

Season: None. Topic: Travel (guide). Link: Travel continues. Word-links: "Cloud" and "sky"; "guide" and "friend".

Season: Mid Spring ([cherry] blossoms). Word-link: "Blossoms" and "cloud". This connection is slight, compared to the earlier links; deliberately Sōgi loosens things up. Also, all the prior verses were written on the opening page, the "face" (that is, more formal part) of the renga. This stanza opens the second page and starts a group of spring verses.

Season: Spring (named). Link: Idea of turning into a bird, to be able to enjoy spring and blossoms from a bird's perspective.

The main feature of all Japanese linked poetry is shifting: Shifting from place to place, action to action, mood to mood. There is no sustained narrative or setting as in most long poems of the European tradition. Special attention goes to shifting from season to season (not usually in order) and out of the seasons into other topics.

Like other classical renga, "Three Poets at Yuyama" connects one stanza to another mainly through word associations common to classical Japanese literature, and through allusions to specific passages in literature. Sometimes an allusion helps to make a link with the previous stanza; other times it provides an opportunity for the following poet to make a link—an opportunity that should not be ignored. In the one hundred stanzas of this renga, for example, thirty or more different allusions have been identified, to works ranging from tanka in imperial and other collections and poems in Chinese by several authors, to *The Tale of Genji* and the Confucian classics. Clearly, one had to study to

kumo o shirube no   with a cloud for my guide
mine no harukesa   the peak's distance

                                            Sōchō

uki wa tada   my gloom is only
tori o urayamu   because I envy the birds
hana nare ya   these blossoms

                                            Sōgi

mi o nasabaya   if only I could change . . .
asayū no haru   spring morning and evening

                                            Shōhaku

write renga. In fact, Sōgi was his generation's greatest scholar of
the *Kokinshū*, much sought-after by his aristocratic patrons for
lectures on the subject.

But renga did not remain in the hands of the aristocratic elite
with leisure to learn vast bodies of classical literature—and the
traditionally recognized pairs of associated words—by heart.
Sōgi himself led the way; he was born of humble parents, in what
province we do not know. He apparently was about thirty when
he came to Kyoto and began studying renga. From this common
beginning he rose to become the preeminent master of renga in
his day. As an apt student of classical tanka, he gained the favor
of highly placed aristocrats and led them at their own game. But
the aristocracy was in decline, and later masters had to find their
patrons elsewhere. In the words of Donald Keene, renga—the
classical variety practiced by Sōgi and his disciples—"is now a
virtually extinct literary art."

Since before the *Kokinshū*, the tastes and aesthetics of the imperial court dominated the Japanese arts. Only certain subjects, diction, and techniques were considered appropriate to serious literature. At the same time, however, many poets were writing about more mundane matters, or using words not native to Japanese, or resorting to unconventional allusions, rhythms, and so on. Almost every era has needed this kind of escape valve to avoid being overcome by refined stuffiness. And more than a few times an outside, humorous, sometimes vulgar literature has set a vigorous new direction for a tradition in danger of sinking utterly in its own pedantry. In court poetry, the word *haikai* was applied to such works in the *Kokinshū* itself, where perhaps the English word "funny" (both "amusing" and "peculiar"—or either) gives a sense of its meaning.

Some scholars believe that the earliest lengthy renga written by aristocratic poets were such poems, involving the less aesthetic details of daily life, Chinese loan-words, and allusions to more popular literature, all excluded from the high-flown poetry that occupied most of their attention in contests, hundred-poem sequences, anthologies, and the like. They say that after a day or evening devoted to serious literary work, the poets would relax and compose renga freely, admitting language and images they would not ordinarily allow, purely for amusement. In contrast with the "heart-full" (*ushin*) courtly style, these poems were said to be "heartless" (*mushin*); considered merely a diversion, they were seldom preserved.

But in the decades after Sōgi Japan went through a difficult time as political power moved ever further from the hands of the aristocrats, and a rising merchant class based in towns demanded the pleasures its leisure and wealth began to make possible. Not able to devote themselves full time to getting the classics by heart, and in any case shut off from participation in the waning literary life of the court, the merchants had little interest in writing high-brow tanka or renga. But some members of the merchant class—especially those who had roots in the warrior class that stood between them and the aristocracy—did want to make a literature of their own. And others of modest birth and unusual circumstances became bridges between the high tradition and the common people. The old *mushin renga* came into public view under the name *haikai renga*.

Often called *haikai* for short, this style of renga was full of new words, images from the lives of the common people, and occasional references to the pleasure quarters, where merchants and samurai alike could enjoy the theater of playwrights like the great Chikamatsu, easy gossip over the events of the day, and the company of the opposite sex.

In this new world of the townspeople the seasons were still deeply important. The annual round of courtly ceremonies had its counterpart in public festivals and religious observances. Agrarian products, still the mainstay of the economy, and the harvests from rivers, lakes, and the sea came and went in their expected months. Human activities, whether work or play, were governed by seasonal variations in temperature and weather. And even the landscapes of cities rarely crowded out the animals and plants today known only to countryfolk. So, one of the most striking features of renga persisted in haikai: the seasons as a source of images and as a primary subject.

The first few decades of haikai produced little work that still brings readers pleasure. The poetry of the commoners, as if to justify aristocratic disdain, was often vulgar and superficial. After the first half of the seventeenth century, however, poets from the merchant class and the lower ranks of the samurai came along who were not content to spend their days teaching and writing a poetry of shallow wordplay that held little interest for anyone but its authors.

The most outstanding of these, Bashō, is still considered by many who have studied the matter to be Japan's greatest poet. Bashō—his pen name—wrote the most important examples of travel-diary literature, and the single poems that are most often quoted. He attracted many of the other poets of his day as disciples, and brought the direct experience of poetry to people scattered widely across his country. In the latter process, he and those who worked with him produced the largest body of linked poetry that is both studied and read for pure pleasure today. Sōgi took the aristocratic renga to its peak; Bashō made over the haikai from a shallow, witty pastime into some of the world's most enjoyable, and challenging, literature.

Since the early twentieth century the Japanese have called *haikai renga* of the Bashō school and later emulators by a new name, *renku*. Renku is linked poetry that focuses on the experiences and language of ordinary people, as did early haikai, but there is a difference. Renku poets seek to represent the full range of humanity and nature in their poems, and link their stanzas mainly through mood and intuition, rather than through simple word associations or esoteric literary allusions. Writing renku is

---

COMMENTARY on Summer Moon

"Summer Moon" (*Natsu no Tsuki*) is a kasen (thirty-six stanza) linked poem in the haikai style, and is also known by the alternate title "Around the Town" (*Ichinaka wa*). The first six stanzas of a kasen appear on the first page, and are usually a bit more formal than later stanzas. The following comments note each stanza's season (with the particular word or phrase that indicates the season in parentheses), the connections and movements between stanzas ("link" or "shift and link"), and an explanation of how the meanings of images and actions change from verse to verse.

Season: Summer (summer moon). The immediate surroundings are suggested, as well as the time of year—as required in the starting verse. Note that the somewhat inelegant opening scene is a bit unusual, perhaps because Bashō, Bonchō, and Kyorai know one another so well.

---

more a measure of a group's humanity than of its erudition and powers of rote memory.

As the quotation at the beginning of Chapter 1 indicates, Bashō also believed in nature as the source of aesthetic value. Like Saigyō, he traveled on foot or horseback through much of Japan, and when not traveling he lived on the outskirts of Kyoto or Edo in modest cottages and guest houses that were loaned to him by his patron-disciples. Though he is known to have studied Zen Buddhism, his devotion to poetry was so great he sometimes complained that his attachment to it would prevent him from attaining enlightenment.

To give an impression of Bashō and companions at their best, here are the opening stanzas of a renku written by the master and two of his closest disciples, Bonchō (d. 1714) and Kyorai (1651–1704). It is variously titled "Around the Town" or "Summer Moon" (a renku of thirty-six stanzas is called a *kasen*):

HAIKAI RENGA: SUMMER MOON
(excerpt, stanzas 1–12)

ichinaka wa   Around the town
mono no nioi ya   the smells of things . . .
natsu no tsuki   summer moon

                   Bonchō

Season: Summer ("It's hot"). Link: The setting is expanded with added sounds and sights. Action added: People cooling themselves outdoors.

Season: Late Summer (second weeds). Shift and link: From town to farm; the verse continues the conversation.

Season: None. Shift and link: Farmer at lunch.

Season: None. Shift and link: Lunch time at a rural shop; a customer tries to pay his bill with a large-denomination coin from the city, which perhaps cannot be changed, and draws attention.

Season: None. Shift and link: Attention shifts to the overlong "short sword" worn by a swaggering youth. Protagonists of both stanzas are self-conscious, a bit boastful.

Season: Spring (frog). Shift and link: Outside at dusk, the youth shies at the sudden croak of a frog in a clump of bushes.

Season: Early Spring (butterburr sprouts). Shift and link: Picking butterburr sprouts, normally a woman's activity, is interrupted by the frog's croak as—startled—she shakes the lantern and it goes out.

atsushi atsushi to	"It's hot, it's hot"—
kado kado no koe	the voices from gate to gate

Bashō

nibangusa	the second weeding
tori mo hatasazu	not yet done, and ears
ho ni idete	out on the rice

Kyorai

hai uchitataku	knocking the ashes off
urume ichimai	one piece of sardine

Bonchō

kono suji wa	in these parts
kane mo mishirazu	silver's an unknown sight—
fujiyusa yo	how inconvenient!

Bashō

tada tohyōshi ni	just extravagantly
nagaki wakizashi	long that short sword

Kyorai

kusamura ni	frightened by a thicket
kawazu kowagaru	with a froggy in it
yūmagure	just at twilight

Bonchō

fuki no me tori ni	picking butterburr sprouts
ando yurikesu	shaking puts the lantern out

Bashō

Season: Mid-to-late Spring (blossom buds). Shift and link: Light going out brings to mind enlightenment.

Season: Winter (named). Shift and link: A monk reflects back upon the austerity of training on the desolate peninsula sticking north into the Sea of Japan. Suggests allusion to an incident in Saigyō's life.

Season: None. Shift and link: The cold poverty of an old man, toothless.

Season: None. Topic: Love (the awaited one). Shift and link: Based on an episode in the "Safflower" chapter of *The Tale of Genji*. The allusion is to the story line, not to particular words: An old woman, cold and having just eaten, admits the prince to her mistress's quarters.

Writing for the newspaper *Nippon*, the upstart poet and critic Shiki Masaoka (1867–1902) chose 1893 to begin a series of columns attacking Bashō. It was, by traditional reckoning, the two-hundredth anniversary of Bashō's death. In the midst of Shiki's continuing tirade, he declared, "The hokku is literature. *Haikai no renga* is not literature. That is why I have not discussed it." (Translated by Donald Keene in *Dawn to the West: Japanese Literature of the Modern Era: Poetry, Drama, Criticism*.)

This violent statement, quoted by others after Shiki had earned his place among the great haiku poets—and written a long essay praising Bashō's "old pond" haiku—helped to push renku into the shadows. R. H. Blyth, writing in the chapter on renku of his *Haiku*, Volume 1 (1949), says:

dōshin no	awakening faith
okori wa hana no	at the time when blossoms
tsubomi toki	are just in the bud

Kyorai

noto no nanao no	in Nanao in Noto province
fuyu wa sumiuki	life's hard in winter

Bonchō

uo no hone	to the point of
shiwaburu made no	sucking on fish bones
oi o mite	looking at old age

Bashō

machibito ireshi	letting in the awaited one
komikado no kagi	key to the side gate

Kyorai

Haikai or renku has practically died out in Japan. The contempt of Shiki for this form of literary composition is often given as the reason for it. . . . Historically, and also for the purpose of understanding their mood and standpoint, the study of haiku needs to be preceded by some acquaintance with the nature of linked verses.

But renku did not die out completely, and even Shiki tried his hand at it. In 1895 and 1896 Shiki and others composed at least four kasen together, one of which he published in *Nippon*. While under medical care after returning from the war in China during the summer of 1895, he composed a one-hundred stanza solo haikai no renga, also published in *Nippon*. And in 1896 Shiki was joined by his two most prominent disciples, Kyoshi Takahama (1874–1959) and Hekigotō Kawahigashi (1873–1937), and others, in writing a kasen called "Thatched Cottage" that was published later

---

COMMENTARY on Thatched Cottage

"Thatched Cottage" (*Kusa no Iori*) is a kasen (thirty-six stanza) linked poem in the haikai style. The opening six stanzas of this poem demonstrate the usual level of calm that prevails at the beginning. The following comments note the seasons and other salient features, stanza-by-stanza.

Season: Summer (luxuriant). Shiki compliments the host through the image of the many shoots (followers) coming up around the tree (host/leader). This accords with the normal etiquette of renku, in which the chief guest writes the hokku using images from the present time and place in such a way as to pay a compliment to the host.

Season: Early Summer (changing clothes). Shift and link: The scene shifts from the courtesies of the front yard to the work area, as Kōroku suggests the axe man has come to trim things up. The phrase "changing clothes" is a season word in the old sense of changing one's wardrobe for the season, but here it is used to suggest getting down to work.

Season: None. Shift and link: Focus shifts from minute detail to broad perspective, from person to setting, a typical method of linking that creates a deliberate break in narrative sequence. Note that occasionally the same poet provides two consecutive verses.

---

that year in *Mezamashigusa*, edited by the major novelist Ōgai Mori.

Bearing in mind Shiki's attack on linked poetry a few years earlier, one might chuckle at the pair of verses by Hekigotō and his master in the opening portion of the renku that follows.

HAIKAI RENGA: THATCHED COTTAGE
(excerpt, stanzas 1–9)

kadoguchi ni   At the gate
nara no shita eda no   under the oak the shoots
shigeri kana   so luxuriant

                     Shiki

koromo o kaeru   he changes clothes
takigi waru hito   the one to split firewood

                     Kōroku

byōbyō to   boundlessly
ta no tsura no kaze no   over the surface of the paddies
wataruran   a breeze wafts

                     Kōroku

Season: None. Shift and link: From one water surface to another.

Season: Autumn (moonlit evening). Shift and link: From the castle as the symbol of higher authority to the village leader as the more local authority. Evening suggests a walk.

Season: Autumn (scarecrow). Shift and link: The face of the scarecrow seen in the moonlight. From walking with some business in mind to puzzlement.

Season: Late Autumn (wild goose). Shift and link: This accounts for the surprise of the preceding stanza. Shiki's disciples no doubt delighted in the notoriety of their leader, and it is hard not to see a wry suggestion here that the goose who normally flies on high has become involved in the swamp of the very literary form he had earlier attacked.

Season: None. Shift and link: As the bringer of the word to the haiku world, Shiki seems to reply that he is tired, and has earned a rest, even in the rustic surroundings suggested by the swamp.

Season: Winter (closes up for winter). Shift and link: One person's solitude (the sleeping messenger) suggests another's (the person sealing the cracks in the ceiling against drafts). Old messages become waste-paper.

ko ni nozo mishi　　beacons seen in the lake
shojō to tomosu　　the castle lights its lamps

                                    Kyoshi

haori kite　　　　wearing light jackets
nanushi e mairu　　we stroll to the mayor's—
yūzukiyo　　　　　a moonlit evening

                                    Shiki

kakashi no kao no　　the scarecrow's face
nani ni odoroku　　what surprises him?

                                    Kōroku

utaretaru　　　　　struck
kari wa ochikeri　　the wild goose has fallen
numa no naka　　　into the swamp

                                    Hekigotō

shisha no yakume no　　the end of a messenger's
hateshi kusabushi　　duty: asleep in the grass

                                    Shiki

fuyugomoru　　　　he closes up
tenjō ni hogu o　　for winter covering the ceiling
haritsumete　　　　with wastepaper

                                    Kōroku

Shiki's continued apathy for renku is demonstrated by the fact that we know relatively few examples in which he participated, while we have tens of thousands of his haiku and tanka. When Blyth spoke of Shiki's condemnation of renku and its supposed demise he was writing during or shortly after World War II and could hardly have anticipated the resurgence of interest in and practice of renku in Japan today. But even in 1946, the respected haiku poet Seiho Awano (1909–93) and members of his group were writing renku. Linked-verse composition in the haikai style, though maligned, never fully died out in Japan.

During the last thirty years renku has been steadily growing in popularity in Japan, and there is now a national organization of renku clubs sponsoring annual events at which the member organizations meet, write, and share their renku.

And renku has become international. In 1992, at the recommendation of Ryūkan Miyoshi, head of the Jigensha Renku Club of Tokyo, a group of six Japanese renku poets toured the United States, visiting California, New Mexico, Wisconsin, New Jersey, and New York. In each place, the members of this Renku North America tour group met with poets from the region and wrote renku with them. An anthology of the more than twenty renku composed during the trip resulted (see Kondō in bibliography).

What happens to the seasons in linked poems? The tension between favored topics and the need for variety has resulted in the development of fixed positions for two very popular images, the moon and cherry blossoms (the latter usually indicated by just the word "blossom"). Also, in both classical renga and popular renku, there are rules about the number of stanzas in a row that can contain images associated with the seasons or with love. The two most popular seasons in Japanese poetry, as seen from an analysis of the older poetry and the way classical poetry collections were organized, are spring and autumn. In linked poems, spring and autumn, once entered, must continue for at least three stanzas, but not more than five. In practice, they usually run for three. Similarly, summer and winter are restricted to no more than three, but more often appear in only one or two running verses.

Another aspect of the way the seasons appear stands out. They do not progress in order, spring-summer-autumn-winter. Rather, they appear in an order governed by aesthetics. Or, as one renku poet put it in conversation with me, you can skip over one season or two to get to the one that is more aesthetically pleasing. Just as important, within a seasonal run the images cannot "back up"—that is, an image from early in the season cannot appear after a mid- or late-season image. But it is acceptable to use an image appropriate to all of the season anywhere within the seasonal run. (Note that in the comments on the renku and renga stanzas above I have used "Spring" to refer to all of spring, and so on.)

That paramount other subject, love, normally occupies from one to three verses at a time, with two being the most common number. Note that it is possible to have a love verse that also reflects a season.

It is said that one does not have a complete renku unless all four seasons and love are included.

The complexity of the rules governing the seasons and love, the moon and blossoms, has led some students of renku to offer charts that show when a given topic may or should appear. Poets in most renku sessions do not haul out charts to justify their proposed verses or to challenge other poets' verses, but such a table may help us to see the results of applying the rules. The most striking result we can observe is that the poem moves in and out of the seasons quite rapidly, just as it shifts quickly from one scene or action to another. The rules promote variety, one of the main goals of renku.

The table on pages 64–65 illustrates the supposed ideal arrangement of the seasonal, love, nonseasonal, and certain other special stanzas on the four pages traditionally used to write out a Japanese kasen (thirty-six-stanza) renku. Based on similar tables in three Japanese renku guides, it has one column for a renku beginning in each of the four seasons. (The special situation of a renku beginning in the New Year period—the first two weeks of January—is omitted here. The three guides are listed in the Japanese sources section of the bibliography, under Obayashi, Okamoto, and Teruoka and Usaki.)

Generally, the table is based on theory and after-the-fact analyses. Like the theories of grammarians about a living language, such analyses have only a limited usefulness to people actually practicing the form. The three Japanese guides also differ among themselves. For example, one seems more flexible than the others about the seasons but very firm on where the love verses should appear—an item that the other two are much more relaxed about. And any group of seasonal verses except the first and last may begin and end a bit earlier or later than indicated. To accommodate the widest variety of practice, I have chosen the most liberal interpretation in cases where the experts disagree.

The column labeled "Special Function" indicates particular content requirements of specific stanzas. Note, however, that the moon stanzas often shift one place or two. When a kasen renku begins in autumn the moon must fall within the first three stanzas, instead of the fifth. The positions of blossom-stanzas, on the other hand, are fairly fixed, though movement, usually to an earlier position, is occasionally allowed.

All sources agree that the first two moon verses should be in different seasons; also, the two blossom verses should exhibit different ideas. Most renku masters will insist on the word "blossom" (*hana*) in the next-to-last stanza, but some will allow "cherry" (*sakura*) in the first blossom stanza, near the middle. In North American practice, "blossom" has often been taken to refer to any of several spring-blossoming trees, and named blossoms are generally admitted, such as "pear blossoms", "hawthorn blossoms", and the like. However, the blossom stanza should not be used for a garden plant or wildflower, which can appear by name elsewhere in its appropriate season. One Japanese source notes that the verse before a blossom stanza should avoid mentioning plants.

Love verses usually gather in pairs, sometimes trios, and their locations are not as fixed as the table suggests, so long as they fall within the first half or two-thirds of the indicated pages. Love verses usually have no season, but may be seasonal.

Renku is one of the most complex varieties of poetry invented so far, and this discussion of the seasons in linked poetry only covers one major aspect of this game-become-literature. Outside of Japan in the late 1960s poets in Paris and Boston, independently, were writing linked poems with some notion of the Japanese tradition. In the last few decades haiku poets around the world have experimented with linked poetry. Most of those experiments have been called "renga", a term that was formerly used for all kinds of linked poetry. During the 1990s, however, growing interest in the details of linked-verse composition and interaction between Japanese and American poets has led to a deeper appreciation of the differences between "renga" and "renku". As it is now understood in Japan, "renga" refers to the aristocratic *ushin renga* of Sōgi and others writing in the courtly tradition of the past. "Renku" means the more popular, intuitive style of linked verse based in the haikai renga of Bashō and his followers and flourishing in Japan today.

It is growing in North America as well. During the 1980s annual workshops in haiku and renku were held at Dai Bosatsu Zendō in the Catskill Mountains of upstate New York. Also in the mid-1980s, *APA-Renga* (now called *Lynx*), a magazine devoted to linked poetry in English, was started in California. Renku composition was a main feature of the twentieth-anniversary gathering of the Haiku Society of America in Spring Lake, New Jersey, in 1988. And in 1990 the Haiku Society of America instituted an open contest with prizes for renku in English. Since the Renku North America tour of 1992, there have been continuing groups of poets writing renku in New York, Pennsylvania, Wisconsin, New Mexico, and California. In 1994 poets in New York, Santa Fe, and California traded renku, or wrote renku collaboratively, with a Japanese renku group based on Sado Island in the Sea of Japan, exchanging their work by facsimile.

63

IDEAL ORDER OF THE SEASONS IN A KASEN RENKU
(horizontal divisions indicate the four pages)

STANZA NUMBER	SPRING RENKU	SUMMER RENKU	AUTUMN RENKU	WINTER RENKU	SPECIAL FUNCTION OF STANZA
1	spring	summer	autumn	winter	compliment host
2	spring	summer	autumn	winter	compliment guest
3	spring	(summer)	autumn	(winter)	break away
4					
5	autumn	autumn	(sum/win)	autumn	moon's place*
6	autumn	autumn	sum/win	autumn	
7	autumn	autumn	(sum/win)	autumn	
8					
9	love	love	love	love	
10	love	love	love	love	
11	(love)	(love)	(love)	(love)	
12					
13	summer	winter	win/sum	summer	moon's place
14	summer	winter	win/sum	summer	
15					
16					
17	spring	spring	spring	spring	blossom's place
18	spring	spring	spring	spring	
19	spring	spring	spring	spring	
20					
21	love	love	love	love	
22	love	love	love	love	
23	(winter)	(summer)	(sum/win)	(winter)	
24	winter	summer	sum/win	winter	
25	(winter)	(summer)	(sum/win)	(winter)	
26					
27					
28					
29	autumn	autumn	autumn	autumn	moon's place
30	autumn	autumn	autumn	autumn	

*Except in autumn, when it must appear in one of the first three stanzas

31	autumn	autumn	autumn	autumn	
32					
33					
34	(spring)	(spring)	(spring)	(spring)	
35	spring	spring	spring	spring	blossom's place
36	spring	spring	spring	spring	optimistic tone

Notes:

Parentheses indicate that a seasonal reference is optional; the verse may be either in the indicated season or seasonless. Unmarked stanzas will normally be seasonless.

The notations "sum/win" and "win/sum" indicate that the verse may be either summer or winter but that once the choice is made, the immediately following verses so marked should be in the same season (or possibly none if in parentheses). If, for example, the sixth stanza in an autumn renku is summer, the seventh may be seasonless or summer; it cannot be winter. Also, once the choice is made for the sixth stanza (or the fifth, if seasonal), the next instance of win/sum stanzas (in this case, numbers thirteen and fourteen) must go to the opposite season, and so on, to create the greatest variety possible.

As international communication by telephone, computer modem, and facsimile continues to increase, and more poets from Japan and outside Japan visit one another's countries, interest in collaborative writing in general, and in renku in particular, will increase. This poetic interaction represents one of the best kinds of sharing and cultural exchange, and suggests that we all may want to look more deeply into the seasons and their representation in poetry.

Perhaps Bashō made a prophesy when he stood on the shore of Honshu and looked out over the Sea of Japan on that famous journey to the "interior" over three hundred years ago:

> *araumi ya*　　　　　wild sea . . .
> *sado ni yokotou*　　reaching across to Sado
> *amanogawa*　　　　the Milky Way

4

HOKKU, HAIKU, AND SENRYU

Chinese poetry, waka, renga, and haikai are all literature.
But even subjects omitted from the first three need not be
left out of haikai.

Dohō (1657–1730), *Sanzōshi*

HOKKU

The opening stanza of a linked poem, the hokku, is usually dedicated to the host, or often to the place of composition and its spirits. (See the hokku to "Three Poets at Minase" page 42.) This means that most renga open in an elevated tone. A renga written without such a dedicatory purpose, however, might begin in a more relaxed way, as does "Three Poets at Yuyama" (pages 42–47). The hokku must always indicate the time of year when the poem is composed. On a more mechanical note, the hokku must also be meaningfully complete, not that it always makes a complete sentence, but that it does not seem to need something more to make sense.

In a confusing way, for years poets used the word *hokku* for the starting verses of renga and renku, and also for verses in the same form that were not used in linked poems. The technical terms "independent hokku" (*jihokku*) and "beginning verse" (*tateku*)—that is, a verse for the beginning of a linked poem—have been used by recent scholars to make the distinction, but were not commonly used by poets.

The practice of writing differently when composing starting verses for linked poems and when composing independent verses began well before Bashō, but he supplies very interesting examples. Bashō wrote the following "hokku" to start a renku in 1689. He had stopped at Tsurugaoka during the journey commemorated in his masterpiece of diary literature, "Narrow Roads of the Interior" (*Oku no hosomichi*):

suzushisa ya	this coolness . . .
umi ni iretaru	Mogami River has put
mogamigawa	into the sea

But in the final version of his diary the poem appears this way:

atsuki hi o	the hot sun
umi ni iretari	put into the sea by
mogamigawa	Mogami River

Bashō worked and reworked his diary over a period of years, only letting it go finally in the summer of 1694, a few months before he died. Why the two versions of this "hokku"?

The first, "this coolness", was used as the hokku of a short renku. Bashō was writing with his companion Sora (1649–1710) and five others, including Fugyoku (d. 1697). Though apparently the renku was abandoned after seven stanzas, one for each participant, the hokku still had to obey the rules: In renku, the hokku must compliment the host and record the time and place of composition. Since the dominant images in the area are the Mogami River and the Sea of Japan, these naturally fall into Bashō's hokku. "Coolness"—a season word for the hot days of summer (roughly equivalent to May through July in the northern hemisphere)—expresses the guest's appreciation for the hospitality afforded him.

Bashō and Sora then stayed a few days with Fugyoku in Sakata, and wrote another renku with him—just the three of them. It was thirty-six stanzas, the usual length for a completed renku at the time. In the final version of Bashō's diary, this later Sakata hokku precedes the Mogami River poem:

> *atsumiyama ya* "Hot-Sea Mountain" . . .
> *fukuura kakete* hanging out at "Breezy Bay"
> *yūsuzumi* cooling at evening

Having written an excellent starting verse for a renku that was prematurely broken off, and a more humorous, though still complimentary, starting verse for a complete renku that would probably be published, Bashō wanted to preserve both the Mogami River and "Breezy Bay" hokku in his diary. But this presented two problems aesthetically: Both the original Mogami River poem and the one on "Breezy Bay" depend on "cool" (*suzu-*) for their effect. In an anthology the two would no doubt be together, but in the context of the diary something other than repetition was needed. And the movement certainly could not be from the seriousness of the powerful river and sea to the light-hearted pun on "Hot-Sea Mountain" and "Breezy Bay". The solution: Reverse the order, so the poems move from the jovial to the serious. And change the key word of the Mogami poem, giving it even more power. Thus was one of Bashō's greatest independent hokku made.

Such independent hokku, written just for themselves or for inclusion in a diary or an essay, had been around for hundreds of years, but it was not until almost 1900 that Shiki, wishing to legalize the separation of hokku from linked poetry, renamed the independent poems *haiku*. Thus divorced, haiku went on its merry way into the twentieth century. Looking at the older poems, one still has to decide whether to call them, as their authors did, *hokku*, or to anachronistically call them, as most moderns do, *haiku*. A third alternative presents itself: Why not continue to call the verses clearly appropriate to starting a linked poem "hokku"—and call the others, obviously meant to be independent, "haiku"? This approach may lead to difficulties, for certainly many verses intended to be independent have the characteristics of a starting verse, while some actual starting verses do not seem to serve a social function. But perhaps looking at a few pairs will help us understand the differences between hokku and haiku in this sense.

Issa (1762–1826), one of the most popular of Japanese poets after his death, and his contemporary Kikusha (1753–1826), both wrote a wide variety of material, including several renku. (There are a few in which they both participated.) Here are two of Issa's hokku which were used to begin renku written with his disciples, the first in 1804 with Seibi (1748–1816), the second with Nabuchi (d. 1834) in 1813:

ima uchishi	The scene just now
hatake no sama ya	as they hit the fields . . .
chiru momiji	the falling red leaves

gohōzen ni	Before the gods
kakate hōzuru	we hang this in offering
hatsu shigure	first winter shower

Japanese and others who love Issa know him for poems such as these:

daimyō o	made the great lord
uma kara orosu	get off his horse—
sakura kana	these blooming cherries

kenka suna	don't fight!
aimitagai no	needing mutual sympathy
wataridori	migrating birds

Issa is the champion of the underdog, the fellow who encourages birds and animals, as in these two independent hokku. But the opening of a renku normally has a more calm, contemplative tone; in the hokku cited earlier the image of the red leaves over the field compliments the host with images of beauty and wealth, and the second poem directly calls itself an offering. In these examples the main differences between the hokku actually used in linked poems and those not intended for such use seem to be in tone; whether in subject matter or language, humor is prominent in the independent poems, and they do not compliment persons, either directly or by implication.

Kikusha, often called Kikusha-ni, was an accomplished artist, musician, and poet, writing tanka, *kanshi* (Chinese poetry), and haikai. She traveled widely, and wrote linked poems with many groups of poets. When she composed a starting verse, it was frequently at the home or temple of a Buddhist teacher. Here are her hokku composed on two of these occasions:

tama ni ge ni	In spirit and in truth
mokutō ya tada	silent prayer . . . just
michi no tsuki	the moon on the road
ogami awan to	To meet and gaze
onaji kumoi no	in the same well of clouds
tsuki hitotsu	at one moon

In the first of these the last line may be understood to mean "the moon of The Way"—a most appropriate reading, since the full moon is often a symbol of pure enlightenment, and the moon in linked poetry is traditionally the full moon of autumn, unless otherwise specified. The "well of clouds" is figurative language for "the sky" and here also implies the world of cares and illusions, with the moon again having its religious overtones. In both instances, and there are others, Kikusha praises the spiritual power of her hosts.

On another visit, Kikusha wrote a verse for her tea-master host, and, though apparently not used in a renku, it also has the characteristic compliment:

tenmoku ni	in the teabowl
koharu no kumo no	this motion of the clouds
ugoki kana	of "little spring"

"Little spring" refers to a spring-like week or two in early winter, similar to North American "Indian summer". The word here translated as "teabowl" (*tenmoku*) literally means "sky-eye", which could be taken as the eye of Heaven, or the eye looking at the sky. It refers to one of the more valuable types of bowls used in the tea ceremony (*cha no yu*). The poem suggests that the tea master's bowl catches the season itself, a high compliment.

It is interesting to contrast Kikusha's treatment of the moon in renku she composed with Buddhist masters, with an earlier verse she wrote on the moon, given in a collection of individual hokku:

tsuki to ware to	the moon and I
bakari nokorinu	alone are left here
hashi-suzumi	cooling on the bridge

"Cooling" (*suzumi*) puts the verse in summer. As noted earlier in connection with Bashō's poems, "cooling" frequently compliments the host of a summer renku. But here it compliments the moon, if anyone, for the poet is clearly alone.

Haruo Shirane, of Columbia University, has noted the extensive commentary in Japanese on this greeting function in haikai literature. In Professor Shirane's translation, the record of Bashō's teaching written by his disciple Dohō tells us:

From the distant past, the *hokku*—called the "guest's greeting verse"—was always composed by the guest as a greeting. . . . [Bashō] taught us that even verses strictly on snow, moon, or cherry blossoms should include the spirit of greeting.

This "spirit of greeting" may be taken as the most important underlying characteristic of hokku. Jumping from Issa and Kikusha of the eighteenth century to the twentieth century, we may see it in the opening stanza of a renku by Seiho Awano (1899–1992):

> *hōkan no*   In a crown's
> *gotoku ni karuru*   likeness, this withered
> *susuki kana*   pampas grass

Here Seiho transforms the wintry image of dried-out vegetation into a laudatory compliment to both beauty and power in the comparison with a crown. The tall silvery fronds of pampas grass provide one of the more attractive autumnal images, as we have seen in the classical renga by Sōgi and his companions in the last chapter. Here again they are carried into winter for a complimentary effect.

This sense of the hokku as a greeting, a blessing, was underlined very recently when the Tokyo renku master Ryūkan Miyoshi published a collection of work by his group, *The Starting Point of Bashō-Style Renku* (*Shōfu Renku no Genten*, 1989). The book contains a pair of kasen renku, two shorter renku, two essays, and two separate sections, one each, of independent hokku and haiku, mostly by Ryūkan himself. A few examples will help us understand what he sees as the difference between hokku and haiku. Here are three of the hokku:

> *mozu naku ya*   a shrike sings . . .
> *eri ashi kiyoki*   clean lines from head to foot
> *toshima kana*   this matron

> *namida seru*   tears come
> *ikusa nagori no*   from memories of battle . . .
> *hiina kana*   these hina dolls

hatsu dayori	year's first letter
mago ni atetaru	addressed to my grandchild
kana no moji	in block letters

In the last of these, *kana no moji* (translated as "block letters") means simple phonetic characters such as those which appear in a child's first reader. Ryūkan, a calligrapher and seal-carver, takes pleasure in greeting his grandchild and in forming the shapes of the characters.

The hokku before, on memories of battle and the courtly figures of March's Doll Festival, expresses the mind of one who has seen dreams for himself and for the empire—implied by the hina dolls that represent the old imperial court—crushed in war. Yet still he—and his compatriots—greet these dolls each spring.

In the first poem the author in effect borrows the song of the shrike, which is more musical than its better-known call, to voice his own praise of an attractive woman. That the shrike tends to travel solo, and comes down from the mountains in autumn to overwinter near populous areas, may add to the meaning.

In each of the hokku just mentioned an aspect of greeting, of interaction between the author and some other, dominates the poem and in effect reinterprets the images to give them a metaphorical meaning beyond their literal significance. And in each the season word itself—first letter, hina doll, and shrike—becomes the vehicle for the poem's "essential meaning" (*hon-i*). Compare these with the following haiku by Ryūkan and one of his closest group members:

se nobashite	I stretch my back
iki o suikomu	and breathe in deeply—
wakaba kaze	a young-leaf breeze

Ryūkan

higurashi ya	evening cicadas . . .
denwa no beru mo	even the telephone's ringing
kiegate ni	fades away

Ryūkan

raiun ni	under thunderheads
kikyō murasaki	the purple of the bellflowers
yurehajimu	begins to sway

Kyōko Kaneko

In all three poems, depth depends on the straightforward presentation of events and reactions to those events, whether of the author or another being, such as the flowers in Kyōko's verse or the telephone's fading in the sweet songs of evening cicadas (*higurashi*).

Kyōko's poem derives part of its power from the way the ominous thunderheads of summer are carried into early autumn, when the Chinese bellflower blooms. There is no overtly metaphorical statement involved.

In Ryūkan's poems the balmy breeze of early summer and the poet's almost instinctive physical response, and the power of one sound over another, need no appeal to metaphor for explanation.

In each of these cases, the meeting of poet and nature is direct, with no hidden meaning to elucidate, no figurative language to figure out. These poems "strictly on snow, moon, or cherry blossoms" serve to uncover the essential meanings of the seasonal images themselves.

TWENTIETH-CENTURY HAIKU

During the twentieth century haiku moved into a new position in both Japanese and world literature. The first part of this change began in Japan during the nineteenth century, when tensions between traditional Japanese literature and the range of new literature pouring into Japan from outside created challenges unforeseen a few generations earlier. This continued through most of the first half of the twentieth century. The second half saw the rise of an international haiku, of haiku written in languages other than Japanese. At the end of the century these two forces are converging to put haiku into a new perspective, both inside and outside of Japan.

Shiki, who was deeply influenced by the independent verses of Buson and their painterly, imagistic presentation, developed a theory of haiku as "sketching from life" (*shasei*). This theory in turn deeply influenced his disciples, many of whom lived well into the twentieth century. It led to a more purely objective haiku, moving away from the metaphorical or symbolic overtones that enriched the work of Bashō and his contemporaries, and even from the sense of greeting. It also diminished the range of haiku content and treatment. Shiki's more than 20,000 haiku hardly span the range of human experience found in Bashō's 1,000 or so hokku, though Shiki's certainly include many more different seasonal references, all told.

Consider, for example, the following, all by poets of the Bashō era, the late seventeenth century:

Bashō ni tsuru egakeru ni　　On a crane depicted in a bashō plant

　tsuru naku ya　　　　a crane cries . . .
　sono koe ni bashō　　by that voice the bashō
　yarenubeshi　　　　　shall be ripped

　　　Bashō

75

A modern haiku poet and critic, Shūson Katō, says of this poem: "As the poet gazed at the painting, he was fired with creative energy and gave free rein to his imagination" (translated by Makoto Ueda in *Bashō and His Interpreters*).

hitorine ya	I sleep alone . . .
yo wataru oga no	as he crosses night the mosquito's
koe wabishi	voice is lonely

Chigetsu (1632–1706)

Chigetsu, missing her husband, projects her loneliness into humor sympathetic to the male mosquito. Perhaps her husband is also "passing through the night" somewhere.

haru no no ni	in the summer field
kokoro aru hito no	that person with deep feelings
sugao kana	and a sober face

Sonojo (1647–1726)

In earlier times, a "person with heart" (*kokoro aru hito*) was one who understood the deep things of life and wrote only serious poetry in the appropriate high diction. Sonojo seems to be taunting such a one for his sober face; as a haikai poet she knows that summer is a time for work, but also for joy.

ishi mo ki mo	trees and rocks too—
manako ni hikaru	in the eyes the light of
atsusa kana	this heat

Kyorai (1651–1704)

Kyorai cannot find anywhere to rest his eyes from the glare of a summer day.

kono aki wa	as for this autumn
hiza ni ko no naki	moon-viewing's without
tsukimi kana	a child in the lap

Onitsura (1660–1738)

This gentle lament for his dead child is by "the other Bashō", a poet whose work includes some of the range and depth of Bashō as well as the wide empathy associated with Issa. Had there been no Bashō, Onitsura might well have been "the first great master of haiku"; most of the best poets of his generation had already apprenticed to Bashō by the time Onitsura, sixteen years Bashō's junior, could have led them.

mishi yume no	seen in a dream
samete mo iro no	even awakening—the color
kakitsubata	of blue flag

Shūshiki (1668–1725)

This is Shūshiki's death verse. She says, in effect, that in this dream of life or awakening in another world, enlightenment is the same.

A similar range might be found among the poems of Buson and Issa and their contemporaries. Shiki, however broad his sympathies in terms of subject matter, including battlefields and his own sickbed, narrowed the range of haiku treatment to a plain presentation, a flat statement verging dangerously close to banality. His most prominent and long-lived disciple, Kyoshi, maintained the trend, heading up the "New Traditionalist" school of haiku poets and founding the magazine and organization known as *Hototogisu* ("Cuckoo"—without the connotations of that name in English). But even Kyoshi allowed himself some room for fancy:

77

itechō no	a chilled butterfly
ono ga tamashii	after its own spirit
ōte tobu	flies off

Before Kyoshi assumed full control of the conservative wing of modern Japanese haiku, Shiki's other leading disciple, Hekigotō, helped lead a revolt in which some poets abandoned traditional form and the imperative to include a seasonal reference, though most of Hekigotō's own poems are not so radical. The "New Trend Haiku" also opened the way to more varied content and treatment, as in Hekigotō's:

danjiki no	while fasting
mizu kou yowa ya	a midnight longing for water . . .
inabikari	rice-lightning

In most contexts one would translate *inabikari* as "lightning flash"; here the characters used to write the word in Japanese are relevant: "rice plant" (*ine*) + "light" (*hikari*). This poem meets all the formal requirements for haiku, but has unusual, and striking, content. The juxtaposition is classic: thin flashes of lightning cut through the dark, paralleling the way desire cuts through the clarity of mind achieved during a fast. Hekigotō was probably conscious of the characters, and recognized the sense of rice as a food plant in the apparently unrelated lightning. An autumn season word, lightning typically occurs at the time of year when rice plants have reached the height of their growth in central Japan.

Hekigotō and others explored the limits of haiku, in terms of form, content, and tone. Here are some examples from the generation that came of age early in the twentieth century.

samui kumo ga isogu	the cold clouds hurry

Santōka Taneda (1882–1940)

Turning his back on most of society, Santōka wrote and lived as he pleased, adopting the premodern role of the begging monk. He ignored form and season words. The word for "cold" he uses here is in the colloquial form, *samui*, rather than the poetic, recognized season word, *samushi*.

furusato o	without even
kou koto mo naku	longing for the old hometown
shōji haru	I paper *shōji*

Midorijo Abe (1886–1980)

Without striving for radicalism, Midorijo shows a quiet independence. Here she rejects the conventional misty-eyed nostalgia about one's childhood home usually associated with this mid-autumn task. She simply repairs her *shōji*, the lightweight sliding doors, made of thin wooden lattices covered with paper, that characterize traditional Japanese architecture.

hi no moyuru	I hug a stone
ishi o idakinu	burnt in a fire—
aki no yume	a dream of autumn

Kanajo Hasegawa (1887–1969)

Dreaminess is not ruled out of haiku, but modern poems may involve a surreal tinge not often found in the older haiku. Originally under Kyoshi's mantle, Kanajo formed her own group in 1930, and later left her magazine to a male disciple. (In the world of Japanese haiku masters, this is a bit uncommon; while women may study under men or women, men have usually studied under men. Most women haiku poets have been considered part of "women's-style haiku"—the subject of numerous books and magazines. Kanajo's male disciples indicate both her importance beyond the world of women's haiku and some cracks in the wall between the male-dominated hierarchy and women's haiku.)

> *mijikayo ya*   the short night . . .
> *chichi-zeri naku ko o*   kid crying in a bid for milk
> *sutetchimao ka*   can I dump the despisèd one?

Shizunojo Takeshita (1887–1951)

In summer not only is the night short, but the poet's child cries right through it. A good part of the power of this 1920 poem appears in the characters themselves. The last line, a very colloquial expression, is written in *kanbun*, the Chinese-style composition of the (typically male) literati, and glossed with the colloquial Japanese pronunciation. (In the translation I have tried to somewhat reproduce the effect by pairing the colloquial "dump" with language echoing Handel.) The haiku poet Kusatao Nakamura (1901–1983) said of this poem:

> No matter how women grasp the new consciousness, aspiring to education and culture . . . each responsibility on top of being a housewife comes to weigh on them. Herein is keenly heard how unbearable the lot of this kind of Japanese housewife . . .

Today's women working in professional and business careers while still carrying primary responsibility for childcare, meal planning, and the like may sympathize. Japanese women still value Shizunojo's often long (for haiku), frequently pithy verses.

Jumping to the present, we find most haiku poets in Japan today still writing in the modes of the early masters, using the literary language, making nature the center of their efforts, observing the traditional formal restrictions, and including seasonal expressions. But the liberating influences of the early twentieth century still echo, and the following poems appear in collections of contemporary haiku.

yuki hageshi	the snow violent
kakinokosu koto	the writings left behind—
nanzo ōki	how come so many?

Takako Hashimoto (1899–1963)

In this, one of her last poems, Takako's own mixed feelings about her illness and impending visit to the hospital come to the fore in the violent weather paired with the wistful, almost child-like questioning.

natsu yasete	thinning in summer—
kirai na mono wa	the things that I hate
kirai nari	I hate

Takajo Mitsuhashi (1899–1972)

It seems that Takajo's deeply subjective feelings become even stronger with the seasonal changes in her body.

genshi yori	since creation
aoumi fuyu mo	the green sea even in winter
iro kaezu	doesn't change color

Seishi Yamaguchi (1901–1993)

Here again, we have the theme of change and permanence, in a psychological, rather than scientific, statement. Significant that the named season itself is the only seasonal reference.

ari korosu	killing an ant
ware o sannin no	I was watched by
ko ni mirarenu	my three children

Shūson Katō (1905–1993)

For Shūson, the stares of children rather than Buddhist precepts strike his conscience.

HAIKU TODAY

Today information and poems flow back and forth between haiku communities in Japan and the rest of the world. Since the mid-1980s there have been at least three books in Japanese about haiku in English, not to mention the reverse flow in German, Dutch, French, Romanian, Italian, and other languages. In 1990 some of Japan's top haiku poets formed the Haiku International Association, issuing their first polylingual journal that December. Called simply *HI*, it contained haiku from twenty-eight countries around the world.

In the meantime, Japanese organizations have sponsored haiku contests in foreign languages for many years. The first that I know of, conducted by Japan Air Lines in 1964, has been followed by international contests sponsored by two Japanese cities, the Modern Haiku Association, and other groups in recent years. One of the oldest ongoing Japanese haiku contests, sponsored by Bashō's hometown of Ueno in old Iga Province, recently opened an English-language division.

Perhaps because worldwide interest in haiku has blossomed most fully in the United States and Canada, English has become something of an international haiku language. As of this writing there are haiku magazines published in Croatia, Romania, and Japan that present each issue fully in both the native language and English. And in Japan a new development has arisen. While foreign visitors and workers in Japan have composed haiku in their own languages for decades, now many Japanese themselves are taking up the writing of haiku in foreign languages. Their independence from the minutiae of traditional haiku in Japanese has resulted in new work, imbued with the spirit of haiku in its homeland and married to the freshness of a new language and a new internationalism. The authors of the following poems have been published as much in the English-speaking world as in their homeland, Japan. They often find themselves translating their poems for a Japanese audience.

try changing to
another color of lipstick—
spring rain

Ikuyo Yoshimura

Slowly I soak
my painful hands
in the hillside spring

Tadeo Okazaki

summer light
returning
with the boomerang

Kohjin Sakamoto

spring rain—
coming out of Sunday church
I become flesh and blood

Yoko Ogino

In addition, Japanese haiku poets with every intention of remaining true to their tradition are now looking at work by foreign haiku poets with a fresh, open attitude. And some important Japanese haiku poets are reaching out personally, commissioning the translation of small collections of their own work for foreign readers. All of this interaction has built a yeasty, vibrant international culture of haiku, amply reflected in the companion volume to this book, *Haiku World*.

As can be seen by the examples, many twentieth-century

83

haiku, whether written in Japanese or other languages, more closely resemble "verses of haikai" (the literal meaning of *haiku*) than the "starting-verses of renku"—the *hokku*. And there is an important place for both haiku and hokku in our appreciation of our natural and social situations. But there are aspects of nature and society not touched by either hokku or haiku.

SENRYU

Another type of poetry, a bit less well known today than haiku but at one time the most popular variety of Japanese verse, also has its origin in linked poetry. While haiku and hokku both usually depend on nature rather than humankind for their images and at least their overt focus, many of the internal stanzas of a linked poem involve humanity directly. This is especially true in haikai renga or renku, where simply following the rules usually produces a poem in which about half of the verses directly refer to people and their concerns.

In Bashō's day, a game that probably originated as a kind of practice for writing linked poetry became a prominent pastime. In this game, variously interpreted as "linking in front of a verse" or "linking to a front verse" (*maekuzuke*), one person proposes a challenge verse and a second offers a "linking verse" (*tsukeku*) in response. By the mid-eighteenth century, only a few decades after Bashō's death, this game had become a routine amusement in tea houses and wine shops.

Here is how it worked: A person acknowledged as a master or judge, called a "marker" (*tenja*), every few weeks had a small group of "front verses" (*maeku*) delivered to several establishments on a route. On the next circuit the master or an agent returned to pick up the responses (each submitted with a small fee), to deliver a new set of *maeku*, and to distribute prizes for the best of the previous round's *tsukeku*, along with printed sheets of the winning verses for sale.

Much of this activity did not produce great literature, but it did provide the middle class with a source of amusement and self-knowledge, the two basic functions of humor. Markers were frequently among the top rank of haikai poets. Bashō's disciples Kikaku and Sonojo were among them. The latter provided the following challenge verse; note the two lines, fourteen sounds in the original, equivalent to a short stanza of linked verse:

shizuka nari keri   become so quiet
shizuka nari keri   become so quiet

Sonojo selected this response, among others:

menugui o   holding a tissue
motte shōji ni   she leans there
yorikakari   against the *shōji*

As with many verses that appear in renku, this one suggests a story that might be continued in a following verse. We can easily imagine the silence of a person, face half-covered with a tearful handkerchief (the original literally says "eye-wipe") clutched tight in the hand, leaning against the flimsy screen for support.

This verse is not untypical of the indirect love verses in a renku. Given a tradition in which love is a frequent subject—a thirty-six-stanza renku normally has four or five love verses—it is not surprising that such a game as *maekuzuke* frequently produced verses about love. But many other human foibles also appear in those poems, and collections have been an important source of information about customs of the times among the common people.

Being a marker turned into a lucrative business as the popular amusement spread through the towns, peaking in the mid-to-late eighteenth century and continuing up to the middle of the 1800s. The ephemeral printed sheets, called "ten-thousand-verse competitions" (*manku-awase*), soon became the sources of larger anthologies issued periodically and containing the best of the local winners.

Manku-awase included a key that allowed one to note the challenge verse to which each of the linking verses had been written, but in the anthologies the challenge verses were omitted, and the linking verses stood on their own. As one can see from the example by Sonojo, once they had served their purpose as an inspiration, the challenge verses really were not needed to make the meaning of the response clear.

There were well over fifty prominent periodical collections of these poems, many running to over twenty issues. By far the most popular were those issued by a marker whose pen name, *Senryū*, became the name of the genre. Early *senryū* were often signed with a pen name, just as hokku and the stanzas of renku were. Anthologies frequently omitted the authors' names; only with the rise of a new sense of individuality in the Meiji era (1868–1912) did authors of senryu begin routinely publishing signed work, though a few pen names do appear in collections edited by Senryū and his immediate successors. (In English the macron in "senryu" is usually dropped.)

While there was no requirement for a seasonal reference in senryu as there was in hokku, many senryu do contain words that have a seasonal meaning, and some senryu collections were arranged much like the model imperial anthology, the *Kokinshū*. The following samples from the popular senryu series begun in 1796, *Gleanings from a Haikai-style Willow Barrel* (*Haifū yanagi-daru shūi*), give a taste of senryu by the seasons.

> *ichinen ni*   each year
> *ichido shindai*   one time the goods
> *yonagete mi*   get sifted through

Early each spring, merchants take inventory to assess the value of their stock. The poem says "get sifted through", indicating also that the broken, shopworn pieces get thrown out. The humor lies in the fact that only once a year do we bother to get rid of the bad goods.

kakitsubata	the blue flag . . .
kaeru wa koe wo	a frog throws his voice
ryo ni otoshi	with backbone

Here the traditional singing frog of spring is seen in summer when he responds to the thrust of nature in the wild irises (*kakitsubata* bloom in June). Part of the fun here is in that sense of thrust, the haiku-like harmony of iris and frog; part of it is in the human projection of that colloquial expression, "with backbone"; and part of the humor comes from the adroit shifting of the traditional spring-singing frog into summer. So while the subjects of this poem come from the typical natural world of haiku, the treatment and the underlying humor come from the humorous soul of the poet. It is that glint in the poet's eye and the colloquial language that make this poem—however haiku-like in initial appearance—senryu. Its humor would beautifully fit the inner world of renku.

kusa-ichi e	to the grass market
makero makero to	saying "cheaper! cheaper!"
hi ga atari	hit by the sun

"Grass market" is a special market fair held through the night before the Bon Festival, in the middle of the first month of autumn (August in the Gregorian calendar). Vendors sell food and implements used in this festival of welcoming the dead spirits. As the sun comes up, latecomers urge the vendors to reduce their prices or risk not selling their goods. This classic senryu captures the greed of the buyer pitted against that of the seller, all for the sake of a "Holy Day"—have you ever bought a Christmas tree on Christmas Eve?

fushi-ana wo	the knot-hole
zatōno miidasu	searched out by the blind one—
samui koto	it's cold

A shiver helps reveal the source of a wintry draft. There is also a suggestion of the whistling sound the wind makes when it finds a hole in the wall. Like some other early senryu, this poem treats its subject in a very straightforward manner, with little hint of the satiric tone that once seemed to define senryu. Though there is a wry humor here, the blind person is not mocked, nor are the rest of us; it is a simple statement. The main thing that makes this a senryu is its colloquial speech, "it's cold" (*samui koto*) instead of something like "how cold it is" (*samusa kana*). Some of today's poets might accept this as a haiku, though others would balk at the colloquial language.

Modern times have brought three major changes to senryu. First, the idea of responding to a challenge verse has gone out of senryu; people now write senryu independent of any challenge verses, the same as others write haiku without any thought of beginning a renku. Second, the old emphasis on satirizing human affairs has shifted a bit; many modern Japanese senryu seem to have more to do with human perceptions and the turns of phrase that embody them than with satire, and in some cases they project human ideas into the natural scene. Third, as with haiku, women make up an increasing proportion of the authors.

Since the mid-twentieth century there have been senryu clubs meeting and publishing in Japan and anywhere large numbers of native Japanese people live, just as there are such clubs for haiku. While some clubs are very local, many have an international membership. Here are a few selections from one issue of *Senryu Swallow* (*Senryū Tsubame*—the bird), published in Japanese in the 1970s in Los Angeles, California:

yōrōkin	social security
fuete kutsu oto	increasing my shoes'
karuku nari	sound lightens

Issen Kurahashi

kusa mushiri	tearing up the grass
inu mo nakama ni	dogs get together
natte jare	in a group and frolic

Megumi Ōmura

senaka kara	in the middle of my back
kyō no atsusa o	I know today's heat
shiru josō	while weeding

Ichiryū Saitō

jaiyanto	the Giants'
saishū kazari	final embellishment—
waku kanko	a rousing ovation

Ryōko Saitō

kakitome ga	registered mail's
todoki geshuku ga	arrival the boarding house
ikikaeri	comes to life

Hinomaru Watanabe

shiba ga nure	the lawn wet
fuyu ga majika na	winter getting close
shinobu ashi	on sneaky feet

Yoshiko Hachiya

These senryu were selected more or less at random from featured groups in the issue. What makes them senryu and not haiku? For some purists, the absence of a season word in many of them. But more important: The first deals entirely with the humor of a human situation: lightheartedness at a small increase in income translates into light-footedness. The second treats the dogginess of dogs in highly colloquial speech. The third perhaps comes closest to haiku, but the focus is on the sense of heat and the labor, rather than on the nature of heat. The fourth has a topical meaning that will probably disappear with the next baseball season. The fifth shows how humans become enlivened with curiosity. And the sixth, while obviously on a seasonal subject, employs a very colloquial expression as a simple—and fresh—metaphor. In all of these, the humor of human perception is the main subject.

For a taste of recent senryu in Japan, here are two poems each from two of today's leading senryu poets:

poketto no   please get
te o dashinasai   your hand out of the pocket—
owakare desu   it's goodbye

haka no shita no   under the man
otoko no shita ni   in the grave I want
nemurita ya   to sleep

Shinko Tokizane (b. 1929)

The first poem sounds like a mother urging a recalcitrant child to get ready to shake hands with someone in parting. The language and the sentiment are as colloquial as anything in William Carlos Williams. The second suggests a mystery; I don't know if the author is mourning her husband or has simply gone into a kind of surreal world. Some of Shinko's poems have a frankly erotic tone, but any erotic tinge here must come from the mind's interaction with the image rather than from the language itself.

chichi haha no   just like
makura no yō ni   Mom and Dad's pillows
yū yakeru   the evening glows

chō ochite	a butterfly falls
tachimachi ķōru	and all of a sudden puddles
mizutamari	freeze over

Yasuyo Ōnishi (b. 1949)

"Mom and Dad's pillows" remind me of Takajo's haiku on "thinning in summer" quoted earlier in this chapter. In both poems, something subjective is hidden from us; we do not know what Takajo hates, or what causes the "glow" Yasuyo speaks of. The tendency toward subjectivity in some modern haiku and senryu has helped to push the two branches of haikai toward each other. But in her butterfly poem Yasuyo adopts a pure senryu tone with the colloquial "all of a sudden" (*tachimachi*), despite the haiku-like images of butterfly and freezing puddles (traditionally associated with spring and winter, respectively).

Any one of the senryu quoted in this chapter might well have been an interior verse in a renku. Certainly none meets the criteria for a starting verse, and only one or two come close to that union of the human spirit with the rest of nature that has come to characterize the best haiku. I might mention here that some senryu, both older and modern, are didactic and general, seeming more like aphorisms or epigrams than what we usually think of as poems. Such verses, unless particularly apt in expression and humorous in effect, seem to me to have little to do with the haikai tradition, but merely reflect a tendency—common to all cultures—in which short verse-forms lend themselves to witticisms and simplistic preachiness. Ben Franklin was not a haikai poet.

THE THREE FACES OF HAIKAI

Hokku, haiku, and senryu each have a characteristic tone and subject matter. Sometimes the tone or the subject matter in a particular poem comes very close to that normally found in another type. Many of today's haiku have more than a touch of senryu about them. Other so-called haiku frequently come close to or even clearly meet all the criteria of hokku, in the sense of "starting verse" and in the metaphorically polite greeting. And some haiku, perhaps unacceptable as such by purists but increasingly accepted by the reading public, have little or no hint of the traditionally required seasonal theme. But despite considerable overlap, it is still usually possible to differentiate among the three types of poems.

In Japan today there is a tendency to accept as haiku the poems of those who identify themselves as—and are accepted into groups of—haiku poets. For senryu it is much the same. Except in the gatherings of renku poets, there is little discussion of the special requirements of hokku as opposed to the broader range of haiku. Some haiku poets may look down on senryu for its abandonment of the seasonal requirement and its colloquial language. And some senryu poets may point to the old-fashioned literary language of many haiku and claim that senryu embodies the true egalitarian spirit of early haikai.

But all three, hokku, haiku, and senryu, derive from renku. Verses characteristic of each may be composed independently, or in the context of making a linked-verse poem. Other contexts abound: sequences of verses on a theme; prose journals or brief essays including poems; poems written for special occasions; poems presented in calligraphy as visual works in a contemplative or festive space. There is a long tradition of viewing these short verses in social and literary contexts that both enhance and are enhanced by the verses' meanings. The Japanese *haikai saijiki*, or almanac of haikai, is such a context.

5

THE HAIKU SEASONS

> Generally, in writing about something one should know its
> essential character. When one does not, curiosities and new
> words dispossess its spirit, and the thing becomes something
> else. . . . This is called losing its essential meaning.
>
> Kyorai (1651–1704)

FROM SEASONS TO SAIJIKI

All traditional Japanese poetry has historically been deeply
involved with nature. Natural cycles, such as the seasons and
the course of love relationships, have long been major subject
matter for composition, the primary source of figurative language,
and a large part of the basis for organizing poetry collections.
According to principles of Japanese poetry well-recognized by
the fifteenth century, certain words and phrases embody ideas
that go beyond their literal meanings. For example, using the
word "blossom" (*hana*), without the name of a specific blossom,
means the blossoms of ornamental cherry trees. For any other
blossom one must specify: "peach blossoms" (*momo no hana*), and
so on. Further, the word "cherry" (*sakura*) always means "cherry
blossoms"—unless one specifies "fruit of the cherry" (*sakura no
mi*). This last is the reverse of the usual English practice, where
the word "cherry" normally means the fruit and to specify the
blossoms one says "cherry blossoms". But in Japanese poetry the
principle goes deeper.

For the Japanese many natural phenomena and human activities and the words and phrases traditionally used to name them immediately bring to mind the seasons in which they typically occur—or become most noticed—along with a whole range of temporally-related images. The effect on the Japanese reader is somewhat like that for a New Englander who reads the phrase "the frost is on the pumpkin": One not only sees the whiteness covering the orange surface of the pumpkin, but also smells the scent of cut-over fields and woodsmoke, feels the nip of frost in the air, and perhaps thinks of a drink of hot apple cider. A friend, when asked what the phrase meant to her, came up with similar images, and without being prompted associated the phrase with Thanksgiving, in late November.

Every culture has phrases, often used in literature, which bring to mind whole complexes of associated images and feelings. Ezra Pound called the use of such phrases "logopoeia", which stimulates "the associations (intellectual or emotional) that have remained in the receiver's consciousness in relation to the actual words or word groups employed" (*ABC of Reading*). In Japanese traditional literature those "words or word groups" associated with the seasons have been particularly appreciated, and even catalogued.

The starting verse of a linked poem must indicate the time of year in which it is begun. To do this, the author of the opening stanza includes a word or phrase naming a recognized seasonal phenomenon. In his book on renga poetics, *The Road to Komatsubara*, Steven D. Carter translates a brief section about starting verses from Sōgi's guide for beginning renga poets:

Things Appropriate to the Second Lunar Month

Pheasants, cherry blossoms, young grasses, to turn soil under, returning geese (this being appropriate to the Third Month as well), hazy fields, the idea of waiting for the blossoms, burned-over miscanthus (or miscanthus on charred fields), the east wind (this carrying over into the Third Month also) . . .

Obviously, pheasants are not present in Japan only in the second lunar month, roughly equivalent to March in the northern hemisphere and the Gregorian calendar. And cherry trees may bloom in March in Kyoto, but in Tokyo it will be a month later. Note that "returning geese" means wild geese returning to their homes in the north, that is, leaving central Japan. "Haze" may rise in summer and autumn as well as spring. And so on. The point is that Japanese (and, for many phenomena, Chinese) poets have celebrated these things at this time of year, usually because people observed the phenomena then and thought they were at their peak at that time. Sōgi could initiate a beginner by offering lists of what are now called "seasonal topics" (*kidai*) appropriate to given times of year. And from such lists the beginner learned that part of the "essential meaning" (*hon-i*) for each of these words or phrases is: The Second (lunar) Month, or mid spring in the traditional understanding of the seasons.

Both Sōgi, in the latter half of the fifteenth century, and Bashō, two hundred years later, presided over collections of linked poems and individual hokku which were organized by the seasons, and within the season by seasonal topics. By the last anthologies of the Bashō school it was common to provide a heading for each new seasonal topic, with poems on that topic following. Usually there was more than one way to express a particular topic. For example, an anthology of the Bashō school published after his death and called *Gleanings from the Seven-Part Haikai Collections* (*Haikai Shichibushū Shūi*, 1699), includes the following four independent hokku under the heading "Cat's Love" (*neko no koi*). Each expresses the spring seasonal topic a different way:

neko no koi	a cat's love
nezumi mo torazu	can't even catch a mouse . . .
aware nari	how touching

Kinpū (d. 1726)

oi-neko no　　　　the old cat
o mo nashi koi no　even without a tail
tachisugata　　　　in love's stance

Hyakuri (d. 1705)

karaneko no　　　　the Chinese cat
mike ni mo kawaru　becomes a tricolor too—
chigiri kana　　　　his pledge

Kifū (dates unknown)

neko no goki　　　　the cat's food dish
awabi no kai ya　　the shell of an abalone . . .
kata-omoi　　　　　one-sided longing

Shūwa (d. 1714)

The first poem repeats the topic literally. The second associates the cat with "love's stance" (*koi no tachisugata*), and the third with a "pledge" (*chigiri*)—the caterwauling of a cat in its mating ritual. For the third it may help to know that the finest specimens of the Japanese bobtail, the domestic cat native to Japan, are commonly called "three-hairs" (*mi-ke*), meaning tricolor. The last verse pairs a cat and a term that literally translates "one-sided thoughts" (*kata-omoi*), referring to unrequited love. In each case the poet freely expressed the essence of a particular cat involved with a potential mate.

We might call this the "natural approach" to seasonal topics. Each poet tried to capture the essential meaning revealed in a particular observation of "cats' love"; the topic was traditional, but the poet was free to find the exact words to express it.

In the three hundred years since Bashō's disciples made their collections, Japanese haiku poets have moved from an anthology with subtitles indicating the seasonal topics to a reference book offering recognized set phrases, called "season words" (*kigo*), to deal with each seasonal topic (*kidai*), with a paragraph of explanation, plus a number of sample poems. The entry for the kidai "Cats' Love" from *The Japan Great Saijiki* (*Nihon Dai Saijiki*, 1981–2), an encyclopedic, large-format illustrated work in five volumes, makes a good example. Here is the full text with romanized Japanese for the kidai and kigo, plus four of the nine poems presented as examples (poets' dates added):

> **CAT'S LOVE** (*neko no koi*) Early Spring. **Cat's mate** (*neko no tsuma* |versions for male and female differ graphically, but not in sound|); **amorous cat** (*koi neko*); **philandering cat** (*ukare neko*); **wanton cat** (*taware neko*); **commuting cat** (*kayō neko*); **cat goes hunting for a girlfriend** (*imogari yuku neko*); **cat's longing** (*neko no omoi*); **cat's pledge** (*neko no chigiri*); **cats mate** (*neko sakaru*); **cat in spring** (*haru no neko*); **pregnant cat** (*harami neko*).
>
> Explanation: Cats, as a rule, begin mating enthusiastically between mid winter |December| and early spring |February|. Several males will woo one female together, giving voice like crying babies, and remaining absent from the house for several days as they go philandering. Restrictions of aesthetic consciousness based in courtly Japanese poetry were relaxed, and selecting this kind of common subject was significant for the new seasonal topics of haikai. In addition to the livelihood category there were other new seasonal topics, but for waka and renga this kind of coarse world was excluded. However, in the world of haikai fun and banter, such undeniably humorous charm is embraced. Since Bashō, poets of the authentic style |i.e., Bashō-style| have much appreciated and written about this seasonal topic. As for domestic cats, in addi-

97

tion to white, black, red, and tricolors there are varieties such as mackerel tabby cats, tortoiseshell cats, tiger cats, and the like.

Kenkichi Yamamoto

mugimeshi ni	on barley meal
yatsururu koi ka	or emaciated love—?
neko no tsuma	the cat's mate

Bashō (1644–94)

koto no o ni	foot tied up
ashi tsunagaretsu	with a string from a koto
ukare neko	the philandering cat

Kitō (1740–1789)

iromachi ya	colorful part of town . . .
mahiru hisoka ni	in midday light stealthily
neko no koi	the cat's love

Kafū Nagai (1879–1959)

koi neko no	the amorous cat
sara namete sugu	licks at the bowl and quickly
naki ni yuku	goes out to cry

Shūson Katō (1905–1993)

These examples of the way poems on "cat's love" are treated in a Bashō-era anthology and a current saijiki can help us understand both the usefulness and a danger of the modern approach to haiku collections.

In the first place, editors in Bashō's day could assume that readers would know the meaning of the phrase "cat's love", but it will not necessarily mean much to a reader who is just discovering haiku today. To one American poet the phrase suggested an affectionate cat, one that perhaps was snuggling up to a person. And she could not understand what made it a spring seasonal topic. The modern saijiki provides such readers an explanation that helps them understand the essential meaning of the seasonal topic "cat's love" and the other phrases associated with it. The poems themselves particularize that essential meaning in words relating a specific experience. So the saijiki is not just an anthology to be read for pleasure, or an exhibit of the works of members of a particular school—though it may be both; it also teaches by explanation and by example.

In most modern saijiki virtually every example poem includes one of the set phrases which have now become traditional. (A simple grammatical change, such as "the cat is philandering" [neko ukareru], is acceptable.) Innovative saijiki editors very likely add phrases from favorite poems to the lists of season words, if the poems do not happen to use the already accepted phrases. But more than once I have heard a poem criticized because the poet used a term that was clearly indicative of the phenomenon, but not already in the list of accepted kigo.

In defense of the kigo accepted in Japanese saijiki, one might note that many of the phrases happen also to be in four or five *on* (the sounds Japanese poets count, which only somewhat resemble syllables). Of the twelve kigo (including the kidai) given above for "cat's love" eight have four or five *on*, and only three have more. This is convenient for poets looking for a phrase to fit into the five-seven-five *on* form typical of hokku, haiku, and senryu in Japanese.

But comparing the poems in the Bashō-era anthology with the kigo listed in the modern saijiki, we see that two of the four poems contain only distant variants of these "traditional" kigo. Had a purist considered these early poems for inclusion in the modern saijiki, they could have been rejected. As it happens, they are two of the more interesting poems in the older book.

The true usefulness of a reference book depends on the knowledge, skills, and sensitivity of those who use it as much as of those who made it. Properly understood, a dictionary is a compendium of the ways people have invented and used words. The saijiki is much like a dictionary, in that it collects the words and phrases poets have used in speaking about seasonal things. But no saijiki, not even the largest, contains all the seasonal phrases ever used; and all the possible ways to speak of seasonal phenomena may not fit into neat phrases which can easily be applied to similar experiences by many other poets.

Perhaps this is why both Henderson and Blyth, while acknowledging the modern Japanese requirement for kigo in haiku, nonetheless neglected to include such a requirement in their initial definitions of the genre, quoted in Chapter 1. In the next chapter I will describe how to avoid the set-phrase trap, and share some of the ways I have used this fascinating kind of book, the haikai saijiki.

And a saijiki is fascinating. As the above entry for "cat's love" demonstrates, each entry in a large saijiki gives natural, historical, and cultural information about the phenomenon named, related words and phrases, and poems as examples. Some saijiki include a few entries without examples, perhaps hoping to encourage poets to write on those seasonal topics, or because no examples of sufficient quality could be found. But usually one reads a saijiki as much or more for the poems as for any other reason.

There are other reasons for having a saijiki. A saijiki organizes the phenomena of each season in a fairly logical manner. The most usual arrangement groups them into seven categories within each season. For example, the categories of the *Japan Great Saijiki* are, with brief descriptions of their contents:

> **The Season** (*jikō*): general climate; reminders of the previous season; solstice or equinox (which is the *middle* of the season); the months; time and length of day; temperature; approaching the end of the season; anticipating the next.

The Heavens (*tenmon*): sky; heavenly bodies; winds; precipitation; storms; other sky phenomena; light and shade.

The Earth (*chiri*): landscape; seascape; fields; forests; streams, rivers, and lakes.

Humanity (*seikatsu*): clothes; food; home; work and school; sports, recreation, and the arts; travel; moods.

Observances (*gyōji*): sacred and secular holidays and festivals; associated decorations, clothing, foods, and activities; death anniversaries (usually of literary persons).

Animals (*dōbutsu*): mammals; amphibians and reptiles; birds; fishes; mollusks; insects.

Plants (*shokubutsu*): blossoming trees; foliage, particularly of trees and shrubs; garden and wild flowers; fruits; other wild vegetation; fungi.

Literally translated, the names of these seven categories are The Season, Astronomy, Geography, Livelihood, Observances, Zoology, Botany. I have given the more descriptive translations above to show that certain words, in a poetry context, have a broader range of meaning than the more scientific literal translations in English suggest. Other authors or translators may use slightly different terminology or categories. But the categories usually start with a list of more general phenomena such as heavenly bodies, weather, and landscape; then shift to human affairs including customs, activities, and holidays; and conclude with specific animals and plants.

Many saijiki, like the *Japan Great Saijiki*, have five seasons, spring, summer, autumn, winter, and the New Year, each with the categories listed above. (In Bashō's day The New Year roughly coincided with the beginning of spring; when Japan adopted the Gregorian calendar, the two-week-long New Year celebration came to be treated separately.) Others may be organized by months, or by the parts of the season—all season, early, mid, and late—and then further divided into categories. Regardless of the organization of a particular saijiki, it will be logical, and indices allow one to find things quickly. But to use a saijiki comfortably, one must know how the seasons have been traditionally understood in Japanese poetry.

THE HAIKU SEASONS AND THE CALENDAR

"Season" is a word for an idea, a notion, a thought based on many specific experiences, collected by a group, and adjusted as members of the group continue to add to their stock of experiences. Different groups living in different times and places have arrived at different notions of the seasons. But all ideas about the seasons derive ultimately from the sun and its effects on the earth.

The longest day of the year we call the "summer solstice" and the shortest we name for winter. Day and night equal each other twice a year, at the equinoxes. The equinox between winter and summer we call the "vernal" or "spring" equinox and that between summer and winter the "autumnal" equinox. The summer solstice and vernal equinox of the northern hemisphere are, respectively, the winter solstice and the autumnal equinox of the southern hemisphere. When the period of sunlight lengthens day by day in the southern hemisphere, it shortens in the northern, and vice versa. The cycle of solstices and equinoxes forms the basis of one system of counting time. Commonly, the word "year" refers explicitly to the length of time from, say, one summer solstice to the next, about 365 and one-quarter days. But there is another heavenly body that marks the passage of time, with cycles of its own.

The moon shines in the night sky, reflecting the light of the sun. Like the earth, only half of the moon receives direct sunlight at a time. As the moon rotates around the earth, we see only a portion of its illuminated half on any given night. The portion we see varies in stages from none or almost none—the "new moon"—to all—the "full moon" revealing the entire side of the moon facing earth. The complete cycle, waxing from new moon to full moon and waning back to new moon, takes about twenty-nine and a half days.

The word "month" originally meant a unit of time from new moon to new moon. Since a number of whole months each with twenty-nine-plus days will not fit evenly into the number of days in the solar year, we have adopted a flexible month of mostly thirty or thirty-one days to make them fit. This solves a problem almost as old as counting time—how to make months and years come out even. However, by doing this we have ignored the original relationship between the phases of the moon and the days of the month.

A lunar calendar common to China and Japan well into the nineteenth century was based on true lunar months, each starting at the new moon. The full moon rose on the night of the fifteenth day, and the old relationship between the moon's phases and the days of the month is still reflected in the Japanese language. The Japanese word normally translated into English as "crescent moon" literally means "third-day moon" (*mikazuki*). There are also words such as "second-day moon" (*futsukazuki*), a thinner crescent; and "sixteenth night" (*izayoi*), the night after the night of the full moon, when the moon is still worth watching, especially if the night of the full moon was clouded over.

The old lunar calendar was loosely oriented to the solar seasons. The year began with the new-moon-day most nearly midway between the winter solstice and the vernal equinox. Spring began on the day actually midway between them. Variations between the two days resulted because of the differences in length between the lunar and solar years. Every few years this difference was made up by adding a "leap month" to the lunar calendar. As a result, the beginning of spring, which depended on the relationship between the sun and the earth, and the beginning of the lunar calendar year, more or less coincided.

The traditional year was divided into twelve seasonal periods based on the solar year but roughly corresponding to the twelve lunar months, according to the following table.

TRADITIONAL SEASONS AND LUNAR MONTHS

SEASONAL PERIOD	LUNAR MONTHS AND JAPANESE TRADITIONAL LITERARY NAMES	APPROXIMATE DATES IN GREGORIAN CALENDAR
Early Spring	1st: Sociable Month (*mutsuki*)	4 Feb—5 Mar
Mid Spring	2nd: More-Clothes (*kisaragi*)	6 Mar—4 Apr
Late Spring	3rd: Growth (*yayoi*)	5 Apr—5 May
Early Summer	4th: Deutzia Month (*uzuki*)	6 May—5 Jun
Mid Summer	5th: Swamp Month (*satsuki*)	6 Jun—6 Jul
Late Summer	6th: Waterless Month (*minazuki*)	7 Jul—7 Aug
Early Autumn	7th: Literary Month (*fumizuki*)	8 Aug—7 Sep
Mid Autumn	8th: Leaf Month (*hazuki*)	8 Sep—7 Oct
Late Autumn	9th: Long Month (*nagatsuki*)	8 Oct—6 Nov
Early Winter	10th: Godless Month (*kannazuki*)	7 Nov—6 Dec
Mid Winter	11th: Frost Month (*shimotsuki*)	7 Dec—4 Jan
Late Winter	12th: Rushing About (*shiwasu*)	5 Jan—3 Feb

The names of the months given here are only those most commonly encountered in old haikai; there are more names for each month, some derived from Chinese. "Deutzia Month" to the Japanese relates to *u no hana*, a common Japanese flower that blooms at that time. The name may also be understood as "Rabbit Month" since *u* is the sign of the rabbit, fourth in the Chinese zodiac. Anyone who has lived in central Japan through the rainy season will relate to "Swamp Month"; "Waterless Month" may be more difficult to accept. "Literary Month" is also interpreted "Letters Month"—as in writing letters to friends.

"Long Month" is an abbreviation for "Month of Longer Nights". "Godless Month" refers to the time when all the Shinto gods were believed to withdraw to Izumo Province for a meeting, some say to determine who would marry whom in the coming year. A month of "Rushing About" comes at the end, as people finish up the business of the old year and prepare for the New Year's celebration, a habit as old and as human as moving the New Year around to suit religious, cultural, political, or economic convenience.

These are the traditional seasons of haiku today, for Japanese haiku poets. While Japan has accepted the Gregorian calendar for commerce and government, and Japanese haiku poets have adjusted by moving the New Year period and making it a season in itself, the haiku world still observes the old seasons.

For perspective on this, consider the short-lived calendar of the French Republic, begun on 22 September 1792, and replaced on 1 January 1806. The months, and their equivalent time periods in the Gregorian Calendar, were:

FRENCH REPUBLICAN CALENDAR MONTHS	EQUIVALENT GREGORIAN CALENDAR TIME PERIOD
Vendémiaire ("vintage")	22 Sep–21 Oct
Brumaire ("mist")	22 Oct–20 Nov
Frimaire ("frost")	21 Nov–20 Dec
Nivôse ("snow")	21 Dec–19 Jan
Pluviôse ("rain")	20 Jan–18 Feb
Ventôse ("wind")	19 Feb–20 Mar
Germinal ("seed time")	21 Mar–19 Apr
Floréal ("blossom")	20 Apr–19 May
Prairial ("meadow")	20 May–18 Jun
Messidor ("harvest")	19 Jun–18 Jul
Thermidor ("heat")	19 Jul–17 Aug
Fructidor ("fruits")	18 Aug–16 Sep
year-end festival days	17–21 Sep

Specifically chosen to ignore any religious significance, these month-names interestingly parallel the old Chinese and Japanese calendar names. Beginning on or near the autumnal equinox, the calendar also celebrated as its New Year the anniversary of the establishment of the French Republic, thus demonstrating the complex interrelationship among calendars, nature, and the civil, religious, and astronomical authorities that promulgate them.

The haiku seasons, each centered on its solstice or equinox, are not so far from our experience as we might think. Our language retains the usages of our ancestors. According to *The Oxford English Dictionary*, "midsummer" is "the period of the summer solstice, about June 21st." Corresponding words from some other Germanic languages are, "midsommar" (Swedish), "midzomer" (Dutch), "mittsomer" (German), and so on. And there is "midwinter"—again, according to the OED: "The middle of winter; specifically the winter solstice, Dec. 21st, or the period about that time. Also formerly applied to Christmas."—as in the carol "In the Bleak Midwinter".

Both "midsummer" and "midwinter" combine with numerous other words to express phenomena associated with the solstices: midsummer fair, midsummer-night, midsummer rose, midsummer chafer (a beetle), midsummer daisy, midsummer madness, midsummer silver (a plant, also called "silver-weed"); midwinter morning, midwinter snow. "Midwinter" is also used as an adjective meaning cold.

While "midsummer" and "midwinter" do not appear as frequently in English as they once did, a flexible view of the seasons still governs many of our activities. In American schools the "spring term" usually begins in January, and the "fall term" in late August or early September. Publishers announce their "fall lists" in May, and list therein books to be published from August through November or later. In the world of merchants, "spring fashions" appear before year-end goods and New Year's holiday attire are gone from the stores. Our view of the seasons shifts conveniently to meet the needs of our activities.

Traditional notions of the seasons focus mainly on cycles of weather and the plants and animals on which we depend for food, clothing, and companionship. We notice "cat's love" during the coldest time of year, but it clearly means new life, the universal sign of spring.

Any organization of the seasons for the saijiki must be somewhat arbitrary. One could certainly organize them differently, and doing so would be very appropriate to latitudes and climates where the cycles of the temperate zone are greatly shifted, as in the polar regions, or simply do not apply, as in the tropics. Any order imposed on nature by humans will fail to account for all variables, and "not work" in some places or at some times. But the traditional Japanese saijiki offers a modest way to group similar experiences together, allowing them to enhance one another, and helping poets and readers identify with one another's experiences across time and space.

Ultimately, poets around the world will no doubt reject seasonal analyses that ignore the facts of their environments. Lately in Japan poets have begun assembling saijiki appropriate to their regions instead of always accepting the dictates of compilers in Tokyo or Kyoto. And creators of saijiki in these two cities have placed the same phenomena in different time periods.

Despite such variations, the seasonal system provides a logical way to organize our perceptions of the objects, activities, and events that we notice at particular times of year. While the reasons for the seasonal placement of many phenomena—specific flowers and fruits, the arrivals and departures of migratory birds, holidays, and the like—are obvious, the placement of some phenomena in the saijiki may seem quite arbitrary. But if we look closely, we often find that tradition has worked in a most logical manner. Two of the well-known seasonal topics most often challenged by those new to haiku are frogs (spring) and the moon (autumn).

Frogs, many will be quick to point out, are with us throughout spring, summer, and autumn, especially in the mild, wet climate of Japan. Japanese poets usually celebrate frogs for their singing, which also goes on for several months, but which begins, and perhaps reaches its peak (depending on the species), in the spring. The Japanese frogs are not alone. Virgil speaks of "frogs loquacious . . . while spring wets the earth"; Thoreau calls them "precursors and heralds" of spring. We have even named one of the most common frogs of the eastern half of the United States "spring peepers" since we rarely see them, but hear "their high-pitched, birdlike *pee-eeep* . . . the collective voices sound like sleigh bells."—March to April in the northeastern United States, according to *Familiar Reptiles and Amphibians* (The Audubon Society Pocket Guides).

The longing for spring that all people living in temperate zones experience finds release in the sudden onset of the frog chorus. A special joy in fertility and its fruits is part of the essential meaning of a substantial number of the phenomena celebrated in the saijiki, especially in spring and autumn.

Even more than frogs and spring, the association of the moon and autumn in Japanese poetics has come under fire from beginners in haiku, especially those who experience the night sky between the walls of city canyons or against city lighting. To accept "the moon" as referring to the full moon unless otherwise specified raises few problems. But why just in autumn? In autumn, especially at the full moon nearest the equinox (mid autumn in the saijiki), the moon rises at its lowest angle, staying close to the horizon for much longer than at other times of the year. Thus the autumnal moon shows off the well-known optical illusion of appearing larger near the horizon than when it is high in the sky. Admittedly, in Japan this also has to do with weather, since autumn frequently brings clearer skies than summer, making the moon and stars much more visible than during the preceding months. But the clearest skies for moon-viewing seem to occur pretty universally in autumn. In life, as in haikai, the essential nature of the moon is best displayed in autumn.

In summary, these phenomena grasp our attention in their

respective seasons. That is their essential nature. In spring there is a hazy moon in Japan and in Japanese haiku; there are also a summer moon, and a cold moon in winter. But if just the word "moon" appears, haiku readers will respond to the unspoken autumn. Meanwhile, there is another major area in which the makers of saijiki and some poets have been at odds.

HAIKU AND SENRYU WITHOUT SEASONS

Until recently all haiku saijiki contained poems arranged according to their seasonal topics. Since saijiki are both anthologies of exemplary haiku and guides for the writing of haiku, the absence of nonseasonal poems in saijiki has helped to solidify the prevailing view among today's haiku traditionalists that the presence of a season word is a defining characteristic of haiku.

But the older tradition of Japanese poetry, while paying homage to the seasons, has always allowed for poems on other topics. Greetings, laments, and poems on love, parting, travel, religion, and other topics have made up a substantial portion of each of the imperial collections, starting with the *Kokinshū*. In Japanese linked poetry the seasons play an integral role in the shape and texture of a poem, but about half of the verses do not reflect the seasons.

For the last hundred years or so some Japanese haiku poets have consistently written their poems without paying attention to seasonal topics. But poems without seasonal topics, such as the few by Bashō and Shiki and perhaps a majority by the four early twentieth century mavericks mentioned in Chapter 1, could not be included in saijiki. Other poets, while using season words in the overwhelming majority of their haiku, have not abandoned their occasional haiku without them. To a reader appreciative of haiku but not deeply familiar with season words, it may be difficult to pick which poem in each of the following pairs has a season word:

onna no ka no	a woman's scent
waga ka o kiite	this scent I'm smelling—
iru nehan	nirvana day

ishi marushi	the stone is round
ishi ni koshikake	the stone I sit on
futokorode	arms folded

Takajo Mitsuhashi (1899–1972)

sasanaki ni	the bamboo cry
samete asa to mo	awakening me—is it morning
higure to mo	or evening?

ryūboku o	over the driftwood
wataru mono mina	the things that pass all
hi o utsu	hit the light

Sonoko Nakamura (b. 1913)

tsukiyo e jazu tobidasu	jazz flies into the moonlit night—
koinrandorii	the laundromat

gyōkō mae no	before the light of dawn
sarii hatameku	a *sari* flutters
yogen ni nite	like an omen

Kimiko Itami (b. 1925)

Takajo was an important member of the generation born at the turn of the century; not all her poems are so subjective. *Nirvana* in the first of these relates to the mid-spring celebration of Buddha's enlightenment. Perhaps the poem records the experience of a breakthrough in her internal sense of herself. The stone poem strikes me as having a summer feeling, but has no traditional seasonal association.

The poems by Sonoko and Kimiko are from the special magazine *Women Haiku Poets of Heisei* (*Heisei Joryū Haijin*) recently published by Mainichi Gurafu. ("Heisei" refers to the current imperial reign, beginning in 1989.) "Driftwood" (*ryūboku*), which one might think a season word associated with the popular seasonal topic "beach-combing" (*shiohigari*), is not. But the "bamboo cry" (*sasanaki*), typical of the bush warbler (*uguisu*) in its winter thicket, is.

And "moonlit night" (*tsukiyo*) in Kimiko's haiku on jazz places it in autumn. Kimiko is the only avowedly modernist poet among these women, indicating caesuras (which I have translated as line-breaks) in her metrically irregular haiku and often not including season words in them. She also writes modern-style poems, which may have something to do with her sense of freedom from traditional restrictions.

Of course, one will not find the second of each of these pairs in most traditional Japanese saijiki.

While Japanese haiku poets have been arguing over whether season words must be included in haiku, outside of Japan the seasonal aspect of traditional haiku has often been understood poorly, or deliberately ignored, and poets have written many fine haiku without taking notice of the season. Meanwhile, writers of senryu both in and out of Japan have little or no concern for whether their poems do or don't contain kigo.

On the one hand, traditional Japanese haiku poets have had little use for senryu, since they cannot *all* be easily catalogued in the traditional seasonal system or included in traditional saijiki. On the other hand, some traditional haiku poets see nonseasonal haiku as senryu, and therefore exclude them from haiku. Circular reasoning may not be logical, but it often works emotionally. Three hundred years ago Bashō would have smiled at such a mess, and gone on writing and growing in his own way. But in the twentieth century a stalemate seems to have resulted, which only now may be slowly breaking up. Interaction between Japanese and foreign haiku poets seems to be part of the trend.

111

Professor Kazuo Satō, once a student of R. H. Blyth and for the past decade or more director of the International Division of the Museum of Haiku Literature in Tokyo, has been tracking overseas haiku for many years. His 1987 book in Japanese, *From Haiku to Haiku* (*Haiku kara HAIKU e*, with the second "haiku" spelled out in English letters), was probably the first to bring world haiku directly to the notice of a broad Japanese public. A few years later New Yorker Hiroaki Sato (no relation) published, in Tokyo in Japanese, *English-Language Haiku* (*Eigo Haiku*), devoted mainly to the haiku scene in North America.

Since all educated Japanese read some English, general interest in English-language haiku is growing in Japan. Some college English-language teachers have their Japanese students write haiku in English, and there are Japanese clubs whose members compose and publish haiku solely in English. When questioned about their reasons for writing haiku in English rather than in Japanese, such poets frequently cite the relative freedom from formal constraints and the season-word requirement.

Meanwhile, in 1989 two ways of side-stepping the seasonal issue arose in Japan. First, a group of radical "New Wave Haiku" poets proposed a new kind of "saijiki", not based on seasons. Second, an important and innovative haiku master added a section of seasonless haiku to his saijiki. And in the same year, a group of Japan's leading poets and scholars published a saijiki including many kinds of traditional poems—haiku, tanka, and others—with a large section of nonseasonal poems.

IGNORING SEASONS IN ARRANGING HAIKU

"An Image Saijiki" (*Imēji Saijiki*), edited by Kōji Yasui and others and published in the June 1989 issue of the magazine *Haiku Space* (*Haiku Kūkan*), preserves the traditional group aspect of a haiku saijiki by arranging poems by categories and topics, rather than by authorship. But the categories and topics are all nonseasonal. Here are the categories of "An Image Saijiki" with their topics:

Living (*ikiru*): human life (*jinsei*), death (*shi*), history (*rekishi*), animals (*dōbutsu*), plants (*shokubutsu*).

Looking for Myself (*watakushi o sagasu*): the body (*karada*), I/me (*watakushi*), children (*kodomo*), juveniles (*shōnen*), youth (*seinen*), old age (*rōnen*).

Work (*hataraku*): trade, occupation (*rōdō, shigoto*), housework, child-rearing (*kaji, ikuji*), capitalism, socialism (*shihon shugi, shakai shugi*).

Leisure (*asobu*): sports (*supōtsu*), the arts (*geijutsu*), travel (*tabi*), consumption and trade (*shōhi baibai*), ceremonial occasions (*kankonsōsai*).

Mingling (*majiwaru*): fighting (*tatakau*), sickness (*yamai*), love (*ai*), sex (*sei*), gods and Buddhas, religion (*shinbutsu, shūkyō*).

Gathering (*atsumaru*): residing, house (*sumu, ie*), family (*kazoku*), cities and towns (*toshi*), villages (*mura*), the nation, Japan, the Emperor (*kokka, nippon, tennō*), foreign countries (*gaikoku*), the globe, universe (*chikyū, uchū*), different worlds (*ikai*).

As with any reorganization of familiar material, the creation of new categories for assembling haiku gives us a chance to see things in a new light. It may be very useful, for example, to read this one of Shiki Masaoka's three well-known death-verses as an "I/me" poem—as it has been placed in "An Image Saijiki"—rather than as a realization of the seasonal theme on the sponge-gourd:

> *hechima saite*   the sponge-gourd blooms
> *tan no tsumarishi* and there's a phlegm-stuffed
> *hotoke kana*   Buddha here

Note that "Buddha" in this context means a dead person; Shiki refers to himself. But one might as easily place the poem under the "death" topic in the "Living" category, since it speaks of a dying person, or under "sickness" in the "Mingling" category, since the sponge-gourd provides a medication for excessive phlegm. The medication was no longer effective for Shiki, so the plants, which had been cultivated for their medicinal value, were now allowed to grow and bloom in his garden undisturbed. In any case, such placement does not detract from the excellence or poignance of the poem, though it may obscure the fact that its author was dying in autumn (when the sponge-gourd blooms).

It may be significant that *Haiku Space* includes a regular column of comments on haiku in English by New Yorker Hiroaki Sato.

Within a year, Banya Natsuishi, who had helped assemble "An Image Saijiki", published his own *Contemporary Haiku Keyword Dictionary* (*Gendai Haiku Kiiwādo Jiten*), with nonseasonal "keywords" replacing seasonal topics. The book's haiku are arranged under 245 keywords, which are explained. They include such terms as love (*ai*), baby (*akanbō*), hole (*ana*), foreigner (*ijin*), younger sister (*imōto*), king (*ō*), music (*ongaku*), hair (*kami*), north (*kita*), time (*jikan*), tongue (*shita*), and so on. While it is organized somewhat differently, the principle behind the *Keyword Dictionary* and "An Image Saijiki" is the same: arrange poems topically, but ignore the seasons in the process.

If the haiku by Shiki quoted above, and others, seem quite arbitrarily placed in "An Image Saijiki", we must understand that such apparent kinks in the "system" indicate the newness of this method, which will no doubt be refined if continued, just as the seasonal saijiki evolved from a simple organization by topics to carefully researched paragraphs with examples under seasonal topics. One criticism of such a reorganization would be that taking a haiku out of the context of seasonal associations, when its author was supremely conscious of those associations, may detract from its meaning—in a limited way. But this criticism may work equally well in reverse: Putting a haiku into a context of seasonal associations which may not have been actively considered by the author may deflect the reader's attention from some other intent of the author. Since several of the poems presented as examples in the next chapter of this book may not have been written with seasonal awareness as a primary consideration, I have to hope that bringing non-Japanese poems into a seasonal context will be at least as illuminating as the efforts of these "New Wave Haiku" poets to take Japanese poems out of a seasonal context may be. At the least, placing poems according to the traditional seasonal associations of their images will help us to understand those associations.

There are two caveats I would offer those of the New Wave. Their arrangements so far seem overwhelmingly focused on the human condition, giving nature and events outside of human concern short shrift. They might want to rethink their categories and topics. Second, a system that insists too much on particular lexical content may encourage the production of uninteresting poems, regardless of the type of lexical categories used. Verily Ezra Pound noted: "Homer did not start by thinking which of the sixty-four permitted formulae was to be used in his next verse." What we may need is not so much a replacement for seasonal topics, but a new attitude toward and method of employing them, as well as a means of extending the system to include an even broader range of experience.

ADDING SEASONLESS HAIKU TO THE TRADITIONAL SAIJIKI

Tohta Kaneko, who earlier in his career did not worry much over including season words in his haiku, published his *Contemporary Haiku Saijiki* (*Gendai Haiku Saijiki*) in 1989. After seasonal topics and haiku in the classic seasonal arrangement, Tohta includes a section headed "Miscellaneous" (*zō*). For centuries, in linked poetry "miscellaneous" has designated verses without seasonal reference, on topics such as love, travel, laments, and so on. We see a vestige of such topics in the systems proposed by the New Wave poets. But Tohta's move, to include nonseasonal haiku under the general heading "miscellaneous" after the seasonal haiku, has a great deal of classical precedent to back it up, while it allows seasonless haiku back into the fold.

Like the rest of his saijiki, Tohta's miscellaneous section is arranged in categories and topics. To give the whole a sense of consistency, he uses five of the same categories found in the seasonal sections, omitting only the first, "the season", and fifth, "observances"—which obviously do not apply. Then he adds two new categories, yielding the following set:

The Heavens (traditional)

The Earth (traditional)

People (*ningen*): head (*atama*), brain (*nō*), hair (*mōhatsu*) . . . fatigue (*hirō*), behavior (*dōsa*), name (*jin-mei*).

Livelihood (traditional)

Culture and Religion (*bunka to shūkyō*): art (*bijutsu*), music (*ongaku*), public entertainment (*geinō*), colors (*shiki*), sounds (*oto*), sports (*supōtsu*) . . . peace (*heiwa*), war (*sensō*), nuclear weapons (*kaku*).

Animals (traditional)

Plants (traditional)

Tohta's method of dealing with nonseasonal phenomena is very flexible, allowing for any additions that may be needed. It makes room for a great deal of material mainly concerning humans, without denying the essential immersion of all phenomena in nature. And Tohta includes among his examples some poems which bear on the topic but do not include traditional set phrases. This more open approach to constructing a saijiki has been very helpful to me as I thought about how to structure an international saijiki.

In the meantime, Japan's leading modern poet, who is also an important scholar of the Japanese poetic tradition, Makoto Ōoka, joined with other prominent scholars such as Kenkichi Yamamoto and Tsutomu Ogata in editing *The Great Saijiki* (*Dai Saijiki*), also published in 1989. This encyclopedic work covers the full range of traditional Japanese poetry from the earliest times to the present day, with examples of haiku, senryu, tanka, and many other types. The four large volumes include two on the seasons and one each dealing with places and with other non-seasonal topics.

In 1990 Tohta was involved with other Japanese haiku poets in establishing the Haiku International Association, trying to foster communication between Japan and burgeoning haiku groups all over the world. And since the 1960s Makoto Ōoka has been reaching out to poets outside of Japan through encouraging translations of modern Japanese poetry into European languages, and perhaps most notably through writing collaborative poems with foreign poets in a modern style loosely based on the Japanese linked-poetry tradition. As with the New Wave poets, here too interaction between Japanese and other poets seems to be correlated with a reexamination of the system.

THE FUTURE OF THE SAIJIKI

For most of the twentieth century, the saijiki has been the most important mode of haiku publication in Japan, culling the best from the monthly magazines and relatively ephemeral collections by individual poets. As long as the vast majority of haiku poets agreed that haiku must contain seasonal references, that has been largely appropriate. But, as noted above, a number of Japanese poets—some of them quite important—have chosen either to ignore the seasonal system entirely or to create works both within and outside of its boundaries. Until very recently, Japanese saijiki have made no provision for including poems that do not conform to the seasonal model.

Both the iconoclastic model of the New Wave—dismissing the seasonal aspect altogether—and the firmly traditional model of Tohta and others—adding nonseasonal topics to the saijiki—make room for poems on any topic. Those writing haiku in languages other than Japanese have generally been unable to conform to a season-word-based definition of haiku because of a lack of extensive information on the seasonal system. Interaction between Japanese and other haiku and linked-verse poets has been increasing rapidly during the 1980s and 1990s, including visits to European countries and North America by groups of leading Japanese poets. Two results of this interaction seem to be a greater tolerance for nonseasonal haiku on the part of the Japanese haiku establishment and an increased interest in the seasonal aspect of traditional haiku among non-Japanese haiku poets. Linked-verse poets both in and out of Japan all seem dedicated to including both seasonal and nonseasonal stanzas in their poems, but find the usual haiku saijiki of limited value.

In the meantime, a portion of the boundary between haiku and senryu has been crumbling, as New Wave haiku poets in Japan have coedited anthologies and appear on national media together with leading senryu poets. And the flood of foreign "haiku" now coming into Japan includes many poems that any person knowledgeable in both haiku and senryu would classify as the latter.

On the Japanese side, such poet-scholars as Makoto Ōoka and Kenkichi Yamamoto have helped further erode the boundaries among genres by creating saijiki that include more than just haiku. And both Japanese and others have turned the lens of the saijiki on literature outside of Japan. The next logical step, it seems to me, is an international saijiki that includes both seasonal and nonseasonal poems on a wide range of topics.

6

TOWARD AN INTERNATIONAL HAIKAI ALMANAC

> The Japanese masters such as Bashō, Buson, Issa, and
> Shiki have been popular internationally because their
> images convey universals of human perception . . .
> It is the human connection, our shared human nature,
> that allows us to appreciate haiku from all cultures and
> backgrounds . . .
>
> Randy M. Brooks
> *Midwest Haiku Anthology*

SAIJIKI OUTSIDE JAPAN

The saijiki has been gradually coming to the rest of the world, as a way of looking at Japanese and other literature, as a guide and anthology for native-speakers of Japanese outside of Japan, and as a possibility for the non-Japanese haiku community.

The first book in English based on the saijiki is R. H. Blyth's *Haiku*, published in four volumes from 1949 to 1952. After the first, background volume, the remaining three consist of a collection of Japanese haiku with translations, all organized by season, and within the seasons by traditional categories and about three hundred seasonal topics. He explains the organization in volume 1, under the heading "The Seasons in Haiku". In his introduction to the second volume, at the beginning of the seasonal arrangement, Blyth says:

> In the *Kokinshū* . . . we find the seasonal classification clearly made for the first time, but it must be noted that with this very virtue comes the lack of spontaneity, the beginning of all artificiality that is ultimately to be the death of all poetry. It is the penalty we pay . . . for seeing the plum blossom as the spring, instead of seeing simply its own beautiful form and colour. . . . The *Manyōshū* gives up its spontaneity and unselfconsciousness to the *Kokinshū*. The genius of Bashō restores a certain enriched simplicity to it, and this again, two hundred years later, is brought to its end at the hands of Shiki.

In a footnote, Blyth says "In Shiki's monumental *Complete Classified Collection of Haiku [Bunrui Haiku Zenshū]*, there is such an excess of system that the poetry is swamped by it. For example, there are no less than fifty classes of fans alone."

Further on, Blyth says "For Bashō . . . the season was the most important element of haikai, not as a principle, but as a mode of intuition, a vaster way of seeing particular things." Working from this point of view, Blyth does not describe and explain the seasonal topics in his *Haiku*, the way a saijiki does, but concentrates on explaining what he sees as the meanings of the poems themselves. This method does, of course, somewhat help to explain the phenomena, but Blyth also adds a substantial bias to the work.

It is hard to see how Blyth could have proceeded otherwise, since many of the poems are about things unknown in the West. But in explaining the poems he so overemphasizes the importance of Zen to haiku that he obscures the fact that each haiku is a piece of literature, an object made of words. In fact, Blyth openly denies that haiku is literature, making his bias known, but fails to see that this leads to a narrow, sectarian view of haiku, rather than opening the full range of the literature to the reader. The haiku tradition is richer and more varied than Blyth's Zen-dominated explanations suggest. Nonetheless, his four volumes were the first real introduction to haiku for many who would later become deeply involved, including myself. We can only hope that the present growth of haiku outside of Japan, and the interaction between Japanese and other haiku poets, will help return haiku to Bashō's "mode of intuition".

Indeed, there is a fallacy in Blyth's assertion about the *Kokinshū*, cited above. The organizing principle in an anthology comes after the fact of composition. And while a tradition that continuously organizes anthologies in a particular way may increase readers' and poets' awareness of one or another aspect of the poems—and thereby have some effect on future composition—it need not stifle poets' creativity in the act of composition, so long as that organizing principle is not arbitrarily exclusive. The great flowering of Japanese poetry reflected in the *Shinkokinshū* does not seem to have been hampered by the fact that the seven prior imperial anthologies were all organized in much the same way.

However, as noted in Chapter 5, the exclusion of nonseasonal poems from twentieth century haiku saijiki has created a bias against poems without seasonal reference, and may have prevented a number of otherwise fine poems from coming to the attention of the majority of poets and readers. Not to mention those poems which were never created or never shared because their authors could not find a satisfactory way to include a seasonal reference. In recent years some members of the Japanese haiku community have moved to expand the saijiki to include nonseasonal material, and part of that movement may have been caused by examining foreign literature and by encountering environments where the traditional seasons of Japanese literature do not apply.

From 1968 to 1970 a group of Japanese scholars published the *English Saijiki (Eigo Saijiki)*, with the English title *An English and American Literary Calendar*. The set was edited by Naritoshi Narita, supervised by Kōchi Doi, Rintarō Fukuhara, and

Kenkichi Yamamoto, with a panel of fifty-three scholars collaborating. A one-volume edition was published in 1978.

The Japanese scholars examined a broad range of British and American literature, seeking words and phrases that would indicate a seasonal consciousness. They did not look at haiku in English, then still in its infancy. The scholars arranged 1,405 entries into the four seasons under the seven traditional categories, and 459 entries into the following nonseasonal (zō) categories: place names; animals; plants; home; clothes; food; transport; education and occupation; marriage and religion; sports and recreation; and myths, traditions, and spirits. The *English Saijiki* provides a good notion of the range of things that one might want to include in such a section. Non-seasonal items account for one-quarter of the book.

One cautionary note arises from an examination of the *English Saijiki*: Some of the examples from British and American literature are placed in seasonal categories that may make little sense in terms of the meanings of the texts involved. Quotations from Shakespeare's play *The Third Part of Henry the Sixth*, including the line "The trembling lamb environed with wolves", and lines from *Venus and Adonis*: "If he had spoke, the wolf would leave his prey/ And never fright the silly lamb that day". find themselves in winter because they include "wolves"—a winter season word. But lambs surely represent spring to English and American sensibilities, even though they do not appear in Japanese saijiki. And in these lines the animals illustrate metaphors, not the actual objects in view; they convey no seasonal meaning to a native-speaker. A number of cited examples in the *English Saijiki* have this problem, including passages from Virgil's *Georgics* (in translation) and Thoreau's *Walden* for the "frog" entry; had the scholars looked a bit further, they might have found more appropriate quotations from these works, as I did in the previous chapter. Thus a system that looks only at the words in a piece of literature rather than at what it says may trap the unwary into making seasonal assumptions that are irrelevant to its meaning, or worse, that obscure its meaning.

Also in 1970, Gyokushu Motoyama, a Japanese-American living in Hawaii, published—in Japanese—the *Hawai Saijiki*. Divided into the traditional four seasons plus the New Year, the *Hawai Saijiki* also has a "miscellaneous" (*zō*), section for animals and plants noticed year-round.

The book deals with one of the most difficult aspects of constructing a saijiki outside of the temperate zone: how to assign seasons. In Gyokushu's system, February through April make up spring; summer occupies four months, May through August; autumn falls into September through November; winter gets only December; and January is given over to the New Year. A prominent seasonal topic of winter is "entering the rainy season" (*uki ni iru*).

In addition to familiarizing his readers with the Hawaiian climate, weather, and landscape, Gyokushu's saijiki provides abundant examples of seasonal topics in the human affairs and observances categories, reflecting the mixture of customs indigenous to Hawaii with those of European and Asian origin, plus many specific to the modern tourist economy. For example, Maui's "Whale Festival", the traditional Japanese "Boys' Day", and United States national "Be Kind to Animals Week" all fall in the same two-page spread.

The seasonal topics in the *Hawai Saijiki* are translated into English and illustrated with haiku in Japanese, apparently all by residents of the Hawaiian Islands. Thoughtfully, Gyokushu also includes the scientific names of most of the animal and plant species not readily known to those more familiar with the temperate zones. Altogether, this provides an interesting and instructive model for a saijiki dealing with a tropical climate (the Hawaiian Islands lie just across the Tropic of Cancer).

One suspects that there are similar saijiki already in print for Brazil and Argentina, to name just two of the many countries where substantial numbers of Japanese émigrés live. While many expatriate Japanese belong to local haiku clubs, only in a few places have those writing haiku in Japanese and people writing haiku in other languages had much interaction. One such place is San Francisco, where a Japanese-American couple, Kiyoshi and Kiyoko Tokutomi, gathered with a number of European-Americans in 1975 to form the Yuki Teikei Haiku Society of the U.S.A. and Canada as an English-language branch of the Yukuharu Haiku Society of California, itself a branch of the society by the same name in Tokyo. (It is no coincidence that the Yukuhara group encouraged the development and publication of the *Hawai Saijiki* mentioned above.)

In 1980 the Yuki Teikei group published its *Season Words in English Haiku*, edited by Jin-ichi Sakuma. This is an alphabetical list of English season words, with romanized Japanese translations and indication of their (very low) frequencies in some English-language haiku publications of the 1970s. It is a little difficult to determine on what basis the season words were assigned to their respective seasons, but generally they seem to be placed according to the traditional Japanese understanding. For example, "fallen leaves" is placed in winter, though most Americans—including most haiku poets who are not familiar with the traditional seasons of haiku—normally understand this phenomenon as autumnal. The list may be useful to those interested in Japanese perceptions of the seasons in English-language haiku of the 1970s, and provides Japanese glosses for some 1,200 season words in English.

In 1991 the growing interaction between Japanese and American haiku poets produced *Nichi-ei Haiku Saijiki: Shiki*. The book also bears an English title: *Four Seasons: Haiku Anthology Classified by Season Words in English and Japanese*. It is edited by Kōko Katō, published by the Kō Poetry Association of Nagoya, Japan. This is two books in one, with Japanese haiku (and some translations into Japanese from English) reading from one end and English-language haiku (and some translations into English from Japanese) from the other. Both are anthologies of haiku listed by season words, arranged in the traditional five seasons and seven categories, though none of the season words is explained (as one normally expects in a saijiki). The English side ends with a substantial unclassified "No Season Word" section, but the Japanese has only seasonal sections. The book aptly celebrates the fifth anniversary of the Kō Poetry Association, which publishes haiku magazines in both Japanese and English.

In French, Alain Kervern has published at least two volumes of selected translations from *The Japan Great Saijiki* (*Nihon Dai Saijiki*) with typical entries and sample poems, somewhat rearranged. *The Otter's Awakening: Japan Great Almanac Volume II: Spring* (*Le Réveil de la Loutre: Grand Almanach Poétique Japonais Livre II: Le Printemps*) appeared in 1990; *The Weaver and Herdsman . . . Volume III: Summer* (*La Tisserande et le Bouvier: Grand Almanach Poétique Japonais Livre III: L'été*) came out in 1992. It is a bit curious that the summer volume is named after the main characters celebrated in the Tanabata Festival, an autumn event in the traditional saijiki. However, the Japanese themselves are confused on the matter, and Tanabata is celebrated at some places in July (late summer), at others in August (early autumn).

Kervern organizes his saijiki translations in order by the parts of the seasons, taking only from the category concerned with general seasonal phenomena in his spring volume, and from that dealing with the skies in summer. In his selection of poems, he represents both older and modern poets, as does his source. The books include the original Japanese for the seasonal topics and the poems. These two volumes, even without anticipating more on autumn and winter, may well constitute the largest collection of Japanese haiku available in French, and the only one that substantially represents twentieth-century poets. Unfortunately, they are produced in limited, letterpress editions, and may not have a wide circulation. The books are, however, beautifully made, and well worth reading. Perhaps they will spark interest in producing saijiki of European haiku.

Many North American haiku poets and editors of anthologies have arranged their books by the seasons, but few have classified the poems by seasonal topics, or attempted anything resembling a saijiki. However, in 1993 California poet Jane Reichhold published *A Dictionary of Haiku Classified by Season Words with Traditional and Modern Methods*, a collection of about 5000 of her own haiku in English, organized into five seasons, seven categories, and seasonal topics. She invented a new category—"Moods"—to take the place of "The Season", and freely adapts seasonal topics to her own understanding. Unfortunately, there is no discussion of the topics, so it is not always easy to follow her rationales for the placement of a particular poem. Had *A Dictionary of Haiku* included some description of the topics, and work by many poets rather than one, it would have been the first genuine saijiki of English-language haiku. It may prove useful in broadening the concepts of the topics and categories of experience in the saijiki.

INTERNATIONALIZING SAIJIKI CATEGORIES AND ENTRIES

The traditional categories of the saijiki—The Season, The Heavens, The Earth, Humanity, Observances, Animals, and Plants—do not signify an attempt to limit the range of haikai subject matter, but rather encourage a comprehensive view of life as the source of that subject matter. A saijiki including poems from many different cultures, languages, and environments will have to include entries on new topics, which can be added to the appropriate categories among existing entries on similar topics. Since the Japanese have been creating saijiki for over a century, many phenomena are already included, and on starting out to build a new saijiki with poems in both Japanese and other languages one soon finds that much of the ground has already been well prepared.

To give a sense of the possibilities, I include here some sample entries as they might appear in such an international saijiki. To better illustrate the range of materials in a saijiki, I have gathered them by category, rather than attempting to duplicate the seasonal arrangement with these few entries. These entries are all variations on similar entries included in this book's companion volume *Haiku World: An International Poetry Almanac*, but there is no duplication of poems between the two books. Each entry is followed by a discussion of its relationship to the category and of its features, particularly noting international aspects.

THE SEASON

NEW YEAR'S DAY, *ganjitsu* (New Year). In the old calendar this was about the beginning of spring, and considered a doubly auspicious day. Now moved to 1 January as a result of the new calendar, New Year's Day is still treated as the beginning of spring by some haikai poets. Note that in English the phrase **New Year's** is often used as a noun, meaning "New Year's Eve" or "New Year's Day"; **NEW YEAR'S EVE** and **NEW YEAR'S EVE PARTY** are mid-winter topics.

ganjitsu no	facing the void
kūhaku ni muke	of New Year's Day
tsuzumi utsu	I beat a hand-drum

Hiryoshi Tagawa, Japan

New Year's Day:
some breaths are long,
some breaths are short.

Stuart Quine, England

"New Year's Day" is a good example of entries focused on the name of a season or of a particular time period within the season; such entries make up a substantial portion of those in The Season category. Since this topic already is included in the traditional

Japanese saijiki, I include its Japanese name (in transliteration or *romaji*) right after the English headword for the entry. The entry briefly explains the place of the topic in the Japanese tradition, and includes equivalent terms in English, with explanations. Finally, related terms that constitute topics in their own right are given, with their season.

> **SULTRY,** *jokusho* (late summer). Stiflingly damp and hot; in colloquial Japanese, *mushiatsui*, in literary Japanese *mushiatsushi*. Also: **stifling heat** (*căldură mare*—Romanian).

Sultry afternoon;
   blowing a grassblade whistle
between two thumbs

Lorraine E. Harr, OR

Căldură mare.	Stifling heat.
O muscă linge ochiul	A fly is licking the eye
peştelui putred.	of the stale fish.

Manuela Miga, Romania

    This entry illustrates another significant subject of The Season category, seasonal temperature. While precipitation comes in the next category, The Heavens, climatic temperature is included here. Again, the corresponding Japanese term follows the headword. Note the part of the season to which this topic belongs, immediately after the Japanese. Nobody means to suggest that sultry weather comes only in late summer (July in the northern hemisphere), but sultry weather has been associated with late summer in the minds of poets for many generations, and those experienced in reading haiku will automatically make that association. Since this is a fairly common and well understood phenomenon it does not require a long entry, but I have included the colloquial Japanese word *mushiatsui*, since many people with only a little Japanese may know it, along with its proper literary Japanese form. The latter, *mushiatsushi*, or the more Chinese-sounding name of the topic itself, *jokusho*, would be used in a Japanese haiku, though a senryu poet would probably use the colloquial form. Finally, the entry includes equivalent terms in Romanian and English, since they occur in a Romanian haiku and its English translation.

THE HEAVENS

SUN, *taiyō* (all year). Seen or unseen, the sun is a constant influence on all life on earth. **AFTERGLOW** (*yūyake*) is a summer topic, but **sunrise, sunshine**, and **sunset** (*ocaso*—Spanish) may come any time of year. **MOON** (*tsuki*), of course, is autumnal. Also: **morning sunshine**.

the thousand colors
in her plain brown hair—
morning sunshine

Bernard Lionel Einbond, NY

sunset
a shoeshine begins
to polish his own

Evan S. Mahl, NY

Torre y ocaso.	Tower and sunset.
Al esplendor del cielo,	On the radiance of the sky,
cuadrado negro.	a black square.

Juan Jose Santander, Egypt

Many of the topics under The Heavens in a typical Japanese saijiki have to do with heavenly bodies of the night sky. Since the sun itself does not appear in a seasonal section, those whose sai-jiki include the sun put it in the nonseasonal section. The inclusion of its Japanese name right after the headword, again, shows that some Japanese saijiki do include such an entry. For some time I have been bothered with calling the nonseasonal section of a saijiki by names like "miscellaneous" (zō) or "seasonless" (muki), so in *Haiku World* I have adopted a more positive name for this section, calling it "all year". The name "all year" parallels "all spring" or "all autumn" in the seasonal parts of the saijiki, indicating that the entries in this section are appropriate topics for any time of year—not defective topics because they are not seasonal. In this entry too, seasonal topics belonging to other time periods such as "moon" and alternative season words under this topic are included, the former in bold capital letters. And again, the season words used in other languages in the sample poems are included. Since this is an international listing, I have added each poet's home state or province, in the case of the United States and Canada, or country after the name.

STARLIT NIGHT, *hoshizukiyo, zvjezdano nebo*—Croatian (all autumn). The Japanese literally means "star and moon night", but is usually taken as referring to starlight; obviously, it does not imply the absence of the moon. **MOONLIT NIGHT** (*yūzukiyo*) is an autumn topic in its own right. A Japanese topic that literally translates as "moonless" (*mugetsu*) means a moon obscured by clouds, and so might best be rendered **CLOUDED MOON** in English.

iznad oltara	over the altar
umjesto krova blista	instead of the roof glittering
zvjezdano nebo	starlit night

Rujana Matuka, Croatia

In this entry the season word of the sample poem is a fairly literal equivalent for the seasonal topic or headword itself, so I have included it at the head of the entry, right after the Japanese topic. Here it seemed useful to explain another topic which might lead to confusion if merely translated literally, so I have included it along with a suggested translation that would avoid the problem. This Croatian poem is a powerful example of this popular traditional topic, and needs no explanation for those familiar with the history of Europe in the 1990s.

SPRING WIND, *haru kaze* (all spring). Includes the early mild breezes and the later bold winds. The Japanese *haru kaze* may also be translated **spring breeze,** if appropriate. **FIRST SPRING GUST** (*haru ichiban*) is a mid-spring topic. Also: **spring gales.**

Cycling along
In the spring wind,
Box of eggs
In my pocket.

Tito, England

spring gales
on the unmade bed
a scrap of snakeskin

Stephen Hobson, Australia

Wind and weather make up about half the entries under The Heavens category. Like most topics that include the name of the season, this one can occur at any time in its season, so it covers a fairly wide range of phenomena. Whereas some terms commonly used in other languages may have readily available equivalents already recognized in traditional saijiki, "spring gales" does not, so no Japanese translation follows it. This is an original season word not previously used in Japanese.

THE EARTH

SPRING FIELD, *haru no no* (all spring). A human mark on the landscape that clearly defines spring, a field between plowing and planting. Also: **plowed field.**

> the warm smell
> of a new-plowed field . . .
> starting my will

Frank K. Robinson, TN

Humans and their creations are as much a part of nature as any other creatures. While many aspects of "humanity" belong in the category by that name, which follows, the landscape abounds with reminders of human presence. In a haiku such human artifacts, and even the action of the author, as in the poem above, are viewed objectively, as one might observe a sparrow's nest. Of course The Earth category also includes many features of landscape and seascape which have no human involvement.

> **ICE,** *kōri* (late winter). Ice may form any time in winter, but indicates late winter in haikai because it seems almost omnipresent then in much of the temperate zone. Also: **icy glaze** (*Glatteis*—German).

> Digging leeks:
> in the viridian whorls
> a nugget of ice.

Padraig Rooney, Japan

Schlechte Gedanken—   Heavy thoughts—
plötzlich bewußt geworden. abruptly brought alert.
Glatteis in der Nacht.   Icy glaze in the night.

          Günther Klinge, Germany

This entry follows the usual format established above. Note that The Earth includes anything that is part of the landscape or seascape, along with ice and its various stationary forms. Icy precipitation comes under The Heavens. In this sample entry the term "icy glaze" is new to the saijiki, so it and its German original are added in the body of the entry without a Japanese equivalent. This haiku has a touch of senryu quality, as the icy street reminds the driver to pay attention to the world, rather than his own woes.

HUMANITY

BEER, *biiru*, *Bier*—German (all summer). Some foods that are consumed year-round still have a strong association with one or another season. Who would deny the special appeal of a cold beer in summer? The Japanese include a number of related terms under this topic: **dark beer** (*kurobiiru*), **draught beer** (*namabiiru*), **beer hall** (*biyahōru*), **beer garden** (*biyagāden*), **canned beer** (*kanbiiru*), to which I would add the related drinks **ale, bitter**, and **stout**. Note that the first poem below seems as much a senryu as a haiku.

'Berliner Weisse!'   'A Berlin Weisse!'
Barfrau vergißt den Sirup, The barmaid forgets the syrup,
sauer schmeckt das Bier.   the beer tastes bitter.

          Guido Keller, Germany

in the Plough's taproom—
furrows on his face fade
as the bitter clears

Jackie Hardy, England

The Humanity category usually starts off with clothes appropriate to the season and then moves to food, followed by house and home, thus dealing with the necessities of life right at the beginning. In this case the entry explains why "beer", which might seem appropriate all year, has a seasonal association. Since beer originated outside of Japan, it is interesting to note some of the related terms already included in the traditional Japanese saijiki. In a commentary on the poems one might point out the relationship between the name of the taproom and "furrows" in the second poem—the saijiki usually assumes that readers are astute enough to notice such things on their own.

TOY KITE, *tako* (all spring). A quintessential toy capitalizing on the winds of March and April. Usually the word **kite** alone is sufficient, but in English the context must make clear that this is not the bird, which is an all-year topic in haikai.

children's voices
rising   rising
with the kite

Jocelyne Villeneuve, ON

After dealing with serious matters such as the necessities of life and work, the Humanity category includes recreation, sports, play, and their many accessories. Note that a possible source of confusion—the existence of another phenomenon commonly found in haikai under the same spelling—is mentioned. To avoid confusion the topic in English is called "toy kite", though the word "kite" alone is usually sufficient in a poem. (I take it that this poem pretty clearly refers to the toy rather than the bird; if the bird were intended the author could have given other clues to clarify the image.)

ILLNESS, *yamai* (all year). Illnesses of many kinds, and the professionals and apparatuses related to them. **COUGH** and **SNEEZE** belong to winter, but **choking** has no season. Also: **clinic, dentist, hospital** (*gasthuis*—Dutch).

As I leave the clinic
   after testing negative—
      the sun and sky

        Tom Tico, CA

every zero
tidily filled in
the dentist's ledger

        Elizabeth St Jacques, ON

Door open deuren   Through open doors
vakken zonlicht en schaduw   squares of sunlight and shadow
in de gasthuisgang.   in the hospital corridor.

        Agnes Verhulst, Belgium

The Humanity category adds various illnesses and other miscellaneous human concerns before finishing up with school-associated activities. Many illnesses and related phenomena are as common at one time of year as another. As these sample poems demonstrate, the topic is large, and we might consider dividing it up into several smaller topics at a later time. Even these few examples show the wide range of affect available in haikai, from the joy of the first haiku to the wry grin of the second poem, a senryu I would say, to the quiet contemplation of the last, a rich haiku.

OBSERVANCES

CHRISTMAS, *kurisumasu* (mid winter). 25 December; commemorates the birthday of Jesus, the Christ. Celebrated 6 January by Eastern Orthodox Christians. Deliberately associated with the winter solstice by early Christians hoping to supplant non-Christian solstice feasts. (The actual birth date of Jesus is unknown.) Aspects of pre-Christian rites remain in the **Christmas tree** hung with **ornaments** and lights, candles, the **Yule log**, bells, evergreen decorations, and special foods. **Santa Claus**, who **comes down the chimney** to put gifts in children's **Christmas stockings**, is apparently based on **Saint Nicholas**, a kindly fourth-century bishop in Asia Minor. The **Nativity scene** or *crèche* displays models of the stable where Jesus was born, the **baby in a manger**, and the parents, animals, shepherds, and **three wise men** or **magi**. **Christmas carols** (*kurisumasu kyaroru*) are sung through the holiday period, especially on **Christmas Eve** (*kurisumasu-ibu*). During the weeks before the holiday, Christians send and receive **Christmas cards** (*kurisumasu cādo*), buy **Christmas presents** for others while **Christmas shopping**, and decorate homes and workplaces. Plants used include **poinsettia**, **Christmas cactus**, and **white narcissus**, as well as evergreens. In North America the period including Christmas, **HANUKKAH**, and **NEW YEAR'S DAY** (part of the separate New Year season in haikai) is often called simply **the holidays**, which in the U.S. may be expanded to include **THANKSGIVING DAY**.

kagi taba o   jingling a bunch
narasu jinguru   of keys in harmony with
beru ni washi   'Jingle Bells'

Shugyō Takaha, Japan

broken ornament
the child's face
in pieces

Barbara Ressler, IA

The Japanese love holidays, and have long included many of European origin in the saijiki along with their own festivals and religious and secular observances. Although the compilers of *The Japan Great Saijiki* do not go so far as to list Christmas among the "500 Essential Season Words" which are especially noted in their work, they include some 40 Christmas poems, making it one of the longer entries. Other holidays imported from Europe and the Americas include Ash Wednesday, Passover, Easter, Hanukkah —even April Fool's Day and Valentine's Day. There are also, of course, many holidays of Chinese, Buddhist, or native Japanese origin included in the saijiki.

> **FUNERAL,** *sō* (all year). All societies have ritualized ways of acknowledging that a person has died. Such rituals may include **burial** or **cremation**; most include prayers or meditations either to help the departed one into the next world or next life, or to assist those still living with accepting the loss. In some religious groups **last rites** are administered while a person is dying or immediately after death; a funeral usually takes place within a day or a few days after the death. When many of those who might otherwise attend a funeral are prevented from doing so by time or distance,

a **memorial service** may be arranged to accommodate their needs. Also: **coffin.**

before the lid
kissing his cold forehead

Linzy Forbes, New Zealand

This entry is from the part of the all-year section of the saijiki that corresponds to the Observances category in the seasonal sections. I call it "Customs and Religion". In addition to the many public and religious observances that fall on particular dates throughout the year—and therefore in particular seasons—there are many functions of a similar ritual nature which may come up at any time of year, such as christenings or naming ceremonies, birthdays, weddings, and funerals. Like holidays, each of these requires us to suspend our usual activities and join with others in a special event. As with the seasonal Observances, each of these events demonstrates our human response to the facts of nature. While some saijiki makers might place the haiku above in the winter section because of the word "cold", it seems to me more relevant to the fact of the funeral than to the climate. Santōka's haiku on sweat, mentioned in Chapter 1, might also be included here rather than in summer, though his focus seems to be as much on the sweat itself as on the funereal aspect; without the prose text that accompanies the poem in the original, or a note, we would not necessarily know that he referred to boxes from the crematorium. These two instances, Santōka's "sweat" and Linzy Forbes's "cold", demonstrate that placement in a saijiki is somewhat arbitrary, and depends to a certain extent on the sensibilities of the compiler.

ANIMALS

CHICKEN, *niwatori* (all year). **Hens** and **roosters** naturally begin mating in late winter, but the laying hen is not allowed much time off from her year-round job of producing eggs. While an "egg" could be that of any bird (or a number of other animals), in many poems the context makes clear that the subject is a **hen's egg**.

always some guilt
laying the hen's egg
in my apron nest

Marian Olson, NM

I like hens
says a peasant woman.
They lay eggs
and are meat too!

Miriana Bozin, Yugoslavia

These two poems illustrate the haikai aspects of an all-year topic like chickens and eggs. In the first example we have an introspective, modern haiku, while the other is pure senryu—aptly demonstrating why we should enrich the saijiki by including senryu as well as haiku.

AMERICAN ROBIN (all spring). *Turdus migratorius*. The world abounds in robins and related birds. The Japanese robin, *komadori* (*Erithacus akahige*), is seen mainly in summer, when it has migrated from south China—and **JAPANESE ROBIN** is therefore a summer season word. The European **robin redbreast** (*E. rubecula*) has been thought of as a spring bird throughout British literature, since it comes back to the Isles in the spring. The American robin, even though overwintering throughout much of coastal and southern North America, is see more in spring and summer. It tends to spend winter in the woods, living on berries, fruits, and

139

nuts, and comes back to farms and towns in the spring to feed on grubs, worms, and insects, when its cheery song announces the beginning of the mating season that characterizes spring in so many species. Probably regions that have robins all year host a more northern-based group in the winter, which moves out as others come in from the south. Though paired in spring and summer for mating, robins gather in large flocks through the winter. I have seen trees full of robins on Christmas Day in the city of Santa Fe, New Mexico. Still, the word **robin** in American poetry will almost invariably be taken as indicating spring, without contrary information in the work.

> there before nine—
> a robin and the bag lady
> working the park

> Carol Dagenhardt, MD

This entry clearly illustrates the need for additional topics in an international saijiki or any saijiki created for an environment outside of Japan. Years ago when I first looked up "robin"— *komadori* according to my trusty English-Japanese dictionary— in a Japanese saijiki, I was dismayed to find it included in summer, rather than spring. A little hunting yielded the information that the American robin with which I was familiar and the *komadori* of the Japanese saijiki are only two of the scores of birds by that name worldwide, each exhibiting its own habits and migratory patterns. So *komadori* may be translated and understood as a summer "robin" in a text dealing exclusively with things Japanese, but for a world saijiki it becomes "Japanese robin" in summer, and is soon joined by the "American robin" and European "robin redbreast"—in spring. Robins from other areas will no doubt cause similar expansions of the saijiki as poems written about them are included.

The saijiki should not be viewed as a fixed canon of acceptable seasonal topics. Rather, it is a flexible system of organizing perceptions, so that poems dealing with similar phenomena may be grouped together, and so that the phenomena they deal with—and the poems themselves—may be better understood and appreciated.

BUTTERFLY, *chō*, *mariposa*—Spanish (all spring). Who has not been charmed by the beauty of butterflies and by their life cycle? In China and Japan one cannot think of butterflies without recalling Chuang-tzu's parable of the man who dreamed he was one. The names of butterflies are legion, and may help to clarify the image: **swallowtail** (*ageha*), **monarch** (*madara*), **skipper** (*seserichō*), and so on. As with many insects and plants, common names can confuse the image. For example, what since childhood I have called a "cabbage moth" (white, with dusky-tipped wings, many with a single small spot in each forewing, day-flying, world-wide) is more correctly a **cabbage butterfly** (Japanese *shirochō*, *Pieris sp.*), for there is a true "cabbage moth" (*Mamestra brassicae*) dark brown with shining white kidney-shaped spots on wings, night-flying, found in Europe, North Africa, and Asia. Butterflies seen in other seasons may be found under the topics **SUMMER BUTTERFLY** (*natsu no chō*), **AUTUMN BUTTERFLY** (*aki no chō*), and even **WINTER BUTTERFLY** (*fuyu no chō*).

De la neblina	Out of the mist
llega con todo su color	comes with all its color
la mariposa.	the butterfly.

Humberto Senegal, Colombia

La mariposa   The butterfly
desconoce que vuela   does not know it flies
entre sepulcros.   between sepulchers.

Ertore José Palmero, Argentina

The last dream of an aged
   fighter pilot—
      butterflies on fire

Elliot Richman, NY

This entry and related topics illustrate one problem in approaching the saijiki. If one only knew of the entry for "butterfly" in spring, it would seem that the saijiki was a bit crazy. For many of the butterflies named in this entry in fact emerge in late spring or early summer in the mid-temperate zones, in haikai terms, so why is this entry designated "all spring"? Well, the first butterflies do appear in spring, some as early as February in milder parts of the temperate zone. For all who are sensitive to seasonal phenomena, the first butterflies of spring are certainly a welcome sign that mild weather has arrived. Also, with Japan's marked rainy season, butterflies become somewhat less noticeable in summer there. But more important, haikai does include and the saijiki does recognize butterflies at all times of year with separate entries for each season, which are also popular topics. We should also note that a number of authorities place the swallowtails (*agehachō*) in their entries for "summer butterfly", some specifying early summer. Shūōshi Mizuhara says that it would not be incorrect to visualize a swallowtail when speaking of a "summer butterfly". Momoko Kuroda correctly includes the striking Japanese emperor (*ōmurasaki*, *Sasakia choronda*)—a purple iridescent with a wingspan of four or more inches (10 cm)—in her list of summer butterflies.

The larger point here is that the saijiki placement of the most generic term for a phenomenon does not exclude the possibility of entries for more specific examples of that kind of phenomenon in other seasons. This especially applies to a wide variety of animals and plants, including several birds, the dragonflies, numerous families of flowering plants and foliage trees, mushrooms, and so on. Even the well-known autumnal scarecrow has a counterpart in the "seed-scarecrow" (*tanekagashi*) set out to protect late-spring plantings. So before one balks at the placement of an entry in the saijiki, it pays to investigate the full range of entries covering closely related topics. Similarly, if a poet asserts that a particular poem involving topic "x" refers to a season other than the one that topic is usually found in, a look through the saijiki may turn up closely related topics in other seasons. During a renku session, verses may be gently revised to help them accord with the appropriate season in such a case.

PLANTS

VIOLETS, *sumire, viooltjies*—Afrikaans (all spring). One of the most traditional signs of spring, the **common blue violet** or **meadow violet** (*Viola papilionacea*) of North America blooms March to June. In Europe the best-known is the similar **sweet violet** (*V. odorata*); in Japan *sumire* (*V. mandshurica*) has a more lavender flower in April and May. There are white and yellow varieties also (some summer-blooming), but the word "violet" will always be taken to mean one of the many blue or "violet-colored" violets of spring unless something else is specified.

Niemand kan sagter　　Nobody rebukes
betig as blou viooltjies,　more softly than blue violets,
niemand harder nie.　　nobody louder.

Hélène Kesting, South Africa

This is another example of a generic word—violet—in haikai referring to a narrow part of its full range of meaning because most people relate first to that more narrow meaning. The number of different species of violets would fill an entire book by itself, but unless one names a particular variety, or says "white violet" or "yellow violet" or "violets in the new-mown hay" or some other more specific phrase, that word immediately brings to mind the blue violets of spring.

> **CHESTNUT**, *kuri, marron*—French (late autumn). The edible fruit of the chestnut tree (*Castanea sp.*). **ROASTING CHESTNUTS** is a late autumn activity in Japan, though Americans may associate it with winter because of "A Christmas Song", which begins "Chestnuts roasting on an open fire . . ." The American chestnut (*C. dentata*) is now virtually extinct, but replaced by Asian species. Not to be confused with the poisonous **horsechestnut** (*Aesculus sp.*), available in late autumn and used in the children's game of **conkers**.

Douceur matinale	Mild morning
Un marron tombe et s'enfonce	A chestnut falls and sinks
dans la boue du parc	into the mud of the park

Patrick Blanche, France

The Plants category encompasses all the seasonal aspects of plants, including for example chestnut blossoms or catkins in early summer and their fruits in late autumn. As with other plants that have noticeable flowers, foliage, or fruits, poets must distinguish which one is spoken of to make the seasonal reference understandable. Since languages differ on whether the name of the plant usually refers to the blossom or the fruit—or the plant itself—and this may vary from plant to plant even within one language, translators must be especially wary in this area. In the French poem above, *marron* definitely refers to the fruit and not the tree (*marronnier*); I hope the translation is as clear. We should also note that when such a word refers to the plant rather than to the flower or fruit, it may well have no seasonal meaning without additional information, for example: "the spreading chestnut-tree" of Longfellow's "Village Blacksmith" suggests no season, but the ongoing force of a life throughout the year and years.

> **LEAVES,** *konoha* (all winter). The Japanese literally means **tree-leaves**. This topic refers to the falling or fallen leaves of deciduous trees, and in many saijiki includes the season word **leaves fall** (*konoha chiru*)— which some authorities place under the related all-winter topic **FALLEN LEAVES** (*ochiba*). The names of the colored foliage and falling leaves of specific trees each have their own appropriate places in the saijiki; we also have the late-autumn topics **COLORED LEAVES** (*momiji*) and **LEAVES RED AND FALLING** (*momiji katsu chiru*), which might readily include the season word suggested in the line from the song, "When autumn **leaves start to fall**".

behind drawn curtains
distorted shadow
of a falling leaf

> Annie Bachini, England

the leaves coming down in it—
the cat's fur parted
to the skin

> Gary Hotham, MD

Again, as this entry suggests, when a seasonal topic seems strangely placed in the saijiki, the great flexibility of the system usually comes into play and allows us to maintain our cherished notions without doing violence to the system. The fact is that Japan's climate is not so different from the climates we experience in other parts of either temperate zone. Generations of Japanese poets' intense concentration on understanding and relating directly to the phenomena of their environment has produced a richly flexible catalogue of human experience, one which yields great pleasure for those willing to plunge into its depths. I hope this foretaste is an adequate preparation for readers who wish to go further on, perhaps in this book's companion volume *Haiku World* and any others of a similar nature which may follow.

HOW TO USE A SAIJIKI

The world of haiku is still the world of a special branch of Japanese poetry. Many of us may write haiku in cultures and climates far removed from the Japanese, but we cannot come close to equaling the number of Japanese haiku poets any time soon. It makes sense, therefore, to capitalize on their centuries of work in developing the haiku calendar, the same as we capitalize on their centuries of work in developing the form, content, and place of haiku in the lives of haiku poets.

This is not to deny that problems will arise, as they have with respect to form and content, for example. Nor is it to say that all must conform to something that makes no sense for their situation. Just as it seems linguistically unreasonable to claim that a five-seven-five syllable form in Chinese or Russian (or German or English, for that matter) closely resembles the form of Japanese haiku, it is naturally unreasonable to expect those living outside of Japan to shoehorn all of their haiku-like experiences into seasons that may be virtually irrelevant to their climates or environments. Still, the saijiki may be a useful way to view haiku and related poems.

Just how useful is a saijiki? I have read saijiki for pleasure, used them as resources to give me a better understanding of the phenomena mentioned in poems, and taken them as guides to help me know seasonal phenomena well enough to write about them accurately myself.

There is the simple pleasure of reading. The Japanese enjoy reading their poems in groups, each poem providing a supportive context for those on either side of it. And who has not enjoyed browsing a book full of information and good poems? Flipping pages in a saijiki, I spot a seasonal topic new to me, or the name of an author I know, or a phenomenon that interests me, and pause to read more. A saijiki can be a fine companion for a few minutes or an entire evening.

Any saijiki is also a critical-historical work, showing off the poems and the tastes of its time. Even though some of the poems in a particular saijiki may not please me, I still get valuable information on what the editor likes, in addition to further knowledge of the topics. Specialized saijiki, for example the *Hawai Saijiki* discussed earlier or Ikuya Katō's *Edo Haikai Saijiki*, may help me better understand the poetry of another place or time. (The Edo era spans the lives of Bashō, Buson, and Issa.) Momoko Kuroda's *Blossoms and Birds Haiku Saijiki* (*Kachō* . . .) has line drawings worthy of a nature guide for almost every plant and animal she includes.

A comprehensive Japanese haiku saijiki is truly an almanac of the natural world and the culture of Japan. Want to know when a particular plant blooms, or what is in flower at a given time? Which fish are commonly available in a particular season? The date of a holiday or festival? When a certain haiku poet died? When to look for polliwogs? What kinds of things get celebrated at different times of year, and why? The history of major cultural events? The saijiki has the answers to these and many more questions. I have often used it to look up references to seasonal phenomena that I found in poems and did not understand.

People who have been writing haiku for some time may feel quite confident that they understand the tradition and what they are doing with it. Poets new to haiku often need some guidance as to how they can incorporate seasonal feelings into their poems. So an anthology including examples of poems that capture the seasonal topics can be a help, if the poems are good and the collection is used properly.

The real job of the haiku poet is to get at the essential meaning of a moment, an event, an object, in such a way that readers or hearers of the poem will be moved to have similar imaginative experiences of their own. Poets have always inspired one another, and what better way to train beginning poets than to offer them a collection of the best in the field? This is what a saijiki is supposed to be.

Almost every haiku master sooner or later edits a saijiki, and some have edited several. Most saijiki come in pocket-sized volumes, some in sets of five—one for each season. For Japanese haiku poets, the saijiki edited by their teacher becomes a sort of bible, a book to carry on haiku walks, a guide to finding the phenomena of a particular time of year. At home, when selecting and revising the rough drafts made on that haiku excursion, the saijiki will help poets understand the nuances of the season words used by other poets. I do not recommend that one slavishly include an existing set phrase in every haiku one writes, but for most beginning poets a saijiki suggests some of the ways one might treat each topic. For more advanced poets, it may illustrate what has been done so that one can move off into new territory.

Until recently, most Japanese saijiki did not help renku poets much. I recall my renku master in Tokyo lamenting the uselessness of contemporary haiku saijiki for renku composition. His two main complaints were that they did not include enough seasonal topics, and that they did not indicate what part of the season a particular phenomenon applied to. The members of his group used a multi-volume saijiki organized by parts of seasons. Their books were several decades old; members had to find expensive out-of-print copies, and the books were falling apart.

Even a saijiki that includes many season words and the part-of-season for each entry still lacks features that could be easily included and which would help renku poets. A nonseasonal section would allow browsing through seasonless phenomena appropriate to renku. The inclusion of senryu, seasonal or not, would broaden the range of treatment as well as subject matter. Including and labeling poems which meet the requirements for hokku, the starting verses of linked poems, would also be quite useful to those writing renku. I have included all these features in *Haiku World*, so that the anthology might be as useful—and as interesting—as possible.

The best and most exciting way to fully appreciate a saijiki is to build one yourself. You can make one on your own or with a group of friends. First, you can collect your favorite haiku and senryu into a saijiki. Reading over the poems and organizing them brings pleasure itself; once assembled, you will find it easy to locate any poem you only partly remember by its topic. A looseleaf notebook or a card file makes an excellent place to keep such a saijiki, allowing easy additions as you discover more favorite poems. You can use the categories and topics in *Haiku World* to help you order the poems, adding your own topics in appropriate places as you find or write poems illustrating them. Keep notes on the topics along with the sample poems, and you can also use your saijiki as a resource for teaching others, perhaps eventually leading to a publishable collection.

Second, and ideal for small clubs and groups that like to write together, make a saijiki for your region with the help of other nearby poets. Start by including poems you and the others have already written, and then see how many additional topics you can find to write about. If you live in an area with notable flora and fauna, locally observed holidays, unusual weather patterns, let them all get into your saijiki. Do not be afraid to include topics none of you has written about yet. Include them, with an explanation, and you soon will.

Using a saijiki may be educational; it is always enjoyable. When you are frustrated because something you think should be there is not, you will begin making one of your own, and learning and enjoying more about both poetry and nature. Whether local, national, or international, a saijiki helps us know both ourselves and our place in the world.

BIBLIOGRAPHY

In addition to the many publications cited in acknowledge-
ments, I have referred to the following works while writing
The Haiku Seasons and compiling *Haiku World: An
International Poetry Almanac*. (I also consulted numerous
field guides and books on customs, animals, and plants, not
included here.) For the works in Japanese, the publisher is
located in Tokyo unless otherwise indicated and names
appear in Japanese order.

WORKS IN JAPANESE

Ebara Taizō, ed. *Kyoraishō, Sanzōshi, Tabineron*. Iwanami Shoten,
  1939.

Fukuda Masahisa. *Bashō, Sekai e*. Amanohashidate Shuppan, 1994.

Higashi Akimasa, Sugiuchi Toshi, and Ōhata Kenji. *Renku Jiten*.
  Tōkyōdō Shuppan, 1986.

Ichiji Tetsuo, et al. *Haikai Daijiten*. Meiji Shoin, 1957.

Inahata Teiko, ed. *Hototogisu Shinsaijiki*. Sanseidō, 1986.

Ishihara Yatsuka. *Haiku no Tsukurikata*. rev. edn. Meiji Shoin,
  1976.

Ishikawa Torakichi. *Senryū Zappai Shū*. Nippon Meicho Zenshū
  Kankōkai, 1927.

Kadokawa Shoten, eds. *Haiku Saijiki*. 5 vols, rev. edn. Kadokawa
  Shoten, paperback, 1972–73.

Kaneko Kinjirō, Nakamura Shunjō, and Teruoka Yasutaka,
  eds. *Renga Haikai Shū*. Shōgakkan, 1974.

Kaneko Tohta, ed. *Gendai Haiku Saijiki*. Chikuma Hansha, 1989.

Kaneko Tohta. *Hyōhaku Sannin: Issa, Hōsai, Santōka*. Iizuka Shoten,
  1983.

Katō Ikuya, ed. *Edo Haikai Saijiki*. Heibonsha, 1983.

Katō Kōko, ed. *Nichi-ei Haiku Saijiki: Shiki / Four Seasons: Haiku Anthology Classified by Season Words in English and Japanese*. Nagoya: Kō Poetry Association, 1991.

Katō Kōko, ed. *Cosmos: Haiku and Renku in Britain, 1992 1.April-4.April*. Nagoya: Kō Poetry Association, 1991. (Largely bilingual Japanese-English, with Japanese predominant.)

Kawada Jun, ed. *Kikusha-ni Haiku Zenshū*. Sara Shoten, 1937.

Kidō Saizō and Imoto Nōichi, eds. *Renga Ronshū Haironshū*. Iwanami Shoten, 1961.

Kubota Jun, ed. *Shinkokin Wakashū*. 2 vols. Shinchōsha, 1979.

Kuroda Momoko. *Anata no Haiku-zukuri*. Shōgakukan, 1987.

Kuroda Momoko, ed. *Kachō Haiku Saijiki*. 4 vols. Heibonsha, 1987–1988.

Matsuyama Shiritsu Shiki Kinen Hakubutsukan. *Kigobetsu Shiki Haikushū*. Matsuyama: Matsuyama Shiritsu Shiki Kinen Hakubutsukan, 1984.

Matsuyama Shiritsu Shiki Kinen Hakubutsukan. *Renga—"Za" no Bungaku*. Matsuyama: Matsuyama Shiritsu Shiki Kinen Hakubutsukan, 1985.

Minagawa Bansui. *Haiku Ginkō no Nyūmon Jiten*. Sanseidō, 1994.

Mizuhara Shūōshi, ed. *Gendai Haiku Saijiki*. Ōizumi Shoten, 1978.

Mizuhara Shūōshi, Katō Shūson, and Yamamoto Kenkichi, eds. *Karā Zusetsu Nippon Dai Saijiki*. 5 vols. Kōdansha, 1981–82. (Called *The Japan Great Saijiki* in the text.)

Motoyama Gyokushu, ed. *Hawai Saijiki*. Honolulu: Hakubundō /Tokyo: Yuku Haru Hakkōshō, 1970.

Nakamura Shunjō, ed. *Bashō Haikushū*. Iwanami Shoten, 1970.

Nakamura Shunjō, ed. *Bashō Shichibushū*. Iwanami Shoten, 1991.

Nakamura Shunjō and Hagiwara Yasuo, eds. *Bashō Renkushū*. Iwanami Shoten, 1975.

Narita Naritoshi, ed. *Eigo Saijiki / An English and American Literary Calendar*. 1-volume edn. Kenkyūsha, 1978 (originally issued as 6 volumes, 1968–70).

Ōbayashi Somahei. *Renku: Jissaku no Chishiki*. Ōtosuraido Purodakushon, 1981.

Okamoto Shunjin. *Renku no Miryoku*. Kadokawa Shoten, 1979.

Okuda Byakko, ed. *Senryū Saijiki*. rev. edn. Osaka: Sōgensha, 1987.

Ōtani Tokuzō and Nakamura Shunjō, eds. *Bashō Kushū*. Iwanami Shoten, 1962.

Saeki Umetomo, ed. *Kokin Wakashū*. Iwanami Shoten, 1958.

Saigyō. *Shinkai Sankashū*. Kita Yoshitarō, ed. Shūbunkan Shoten, 1924.

Sasa Seisetsu and Iwatani Sanami, eds. *Bashō-o Zenshū*. rev. edn. Hakubunkan, 1919.

Satō Hiroaki. *Eigo Haiku*. Simul Press, 1987.

Satō Hiroaki. *Manhattan Karuchaa Sukūru / Manhattan Culture School*. Furii Puresu Sābisu, 1990.

Satō Kazuo. *Haiku kara HAIKU e—Bei-Ei ni Akeru Haiku no Juyō*. Nan'un-do Publishing Co., 1987.

Sawaki Kin'ichi, ed. *Ayako Haiku Saijiki*. Tōkyō Shinbun Shuppankyoku, 1994.

Shimazu Tadao. *Rengashū*. Shinchōsha, 1979.

Sugimoto Nagashige and Giichirō Hamada. *Senryū Kyōkashū*. Iwanami Shoten, 1958.

Sugiura Shōichirō, et al, eds. *Bashō Bunshū*. Iwanami Shoten, 1959.

Tada Michitarō, ed. *Hirune Saijiki*. Chikuma Shobō, 1993.

Takagi Ichinosuke, Gomi Tomohide, and Ōno Susumu, eds. *Manyōshū*. 4 vols. Iwanami Shoten, 1957–1964.

Takagi Sōgo. *Haikai Jinmei Jiten*. Meiji Shoin, 1960.

Takahama Kyoshi. *Kiyose*. rev. edn., Takahama Toshio, ed. Sanseidō, 1964.

Teruoka Yasutaka and Kawashima Tsuyu, eds. *Buson-shū Issashū*. Iwanami Shoten, 1959.

Teruoka Yasutaka and Usaki Fuyuo. *Renku no Susume*. Kirihara Shoten, 1991.

Tomiyasu Fūsei, et al, eds. *Haiku Saijiki.* 5 vols. Heibonsha, 1959.

Ueno Sachiko. *Kindai no Joryū Haiku.* Ōfūsha, 1978.

Yamamoto Kenkichi, ed. *Haiku Kanshō Saijiki.* Kadokawa Shoten, 1993.

Yamamoto Kenkichi, ed. *Kuka Saijiki.* 4 vols. Shinchōsha, 1986, paperback edn., 1993.

Yamamoto Kenkichi, ed. *Saishin Haiku Saijiki.* 5 vols. Bungei-shunjū, 1971–72, and paperback edn., 1977. (Contents differ.)

Yasui Kōji, et al, eds. "Imēji saijiki," in *Haiku Kūkan*, No. 9 (June 1989).

WORKS IN EUROPEAN LANGUAGES

Araki, Tadao, ed. *Symposium zur Haiku- und Renku-Dichtung, 22. Juni 1991.* Cologne: The Japan Foundation, n.d.

Araki, Tadao, ed. *Symposium zur Haiku- und Renku-Dichtung, 23. Mai 1992.* Cologne: The Japan Foundation, n.d.

Beichman, Janine. *Masaoka Shiki.* Boston: Twayne, 1982.

Blyth, R. H. *Senryu: Japanese Satirical Verses.* Tokyo: Hokuseido, 1949

Blyth, R. H. *Haiku.* 4 vols. Tokyo: Hokuseido, 1949–52.

Blyth, R. H. *Japanese Life and Character in Senryu.* Tokyo: Hokuseido, 1960.

Blyth, R. H. *Edo Satirical Verse Anthologies.* Tokyo: Hokuseido, 1961.

Blyth, R. H. *A History of Haiku.* 2 vols. Tokyo: Hokuseido, 1963–64.

Bowers, Faubion, ed. *The Tradition of Classic Haiku.* New York: Dover, 1996.

Brower, Robert H., trans. *Fujiwara Teika's* Hundred-Poem Sequence of the Shōji Era, *1200.* Tokyo: Sophia U., 1978.

Brower, Robert H. and Earl Miner. *Japanese Court Poetry.* Stanford: Stanford U. Press, 1961.

Brower, Robert H. and Earl Miner, trans. *Fujiwara Teika's Superior Poems of Our Time: A Thirteenth Century Poetic Treatise and Sequence.* Stanford: Stanford U. Press, 1967.

Carter, Steven D. "Three Poets at Yuyama: Sōgi and *Yuyama Sangin Hyakuin*, 1491," *Monumenta Nipponica*. XXXIII: 2, 119–149; XXXIII: 3, 241–283 (Summer and Autumn 1978).

Carter, Steven D. *The Road to Komatsubara: A Classical Reading of the Renga Hyakuin*. Cambridge, Massachusetts: Council on East Asian Studies, 1987.

Carter, Steven D., ed. *Traditional Japanese Poetry: An Anthology*. Stanford: Stanford U. Press, 1991.

Fujiwara, Noboru, trans. *A Selection from the Poems of Seishi* |Yamaguchi|. Osaka: privately printed, 1988.

Fister, Patricia. *Japanese Women Artists 1600–1900*. Lawrence, Kansas: Spencer Museum of Art and New York: Harper & Row, 1988.

Furuta, Soichi, trans. *Cape Jasmine and Pomegranates: the Free-Meter Haiku of Ippekiro*. New York: Grossman, 1974.

Haiku Society of America Twentieth Anniversary Book Committee. *A Haiku Path: The Haiku Society of America 1968–1988*. New York: Haiku Society of America, 1994.

Henderson, Harold Gould. *The Bamboo Broom: An Introduction to Japanese Haiku*. Boston: Houghton Mifflin Co., 1934.

Henderson, Harold G. *An Introduction to Haiku: An Anthology of Poems from Bashō to Shiki*. New York: Doubleday Anchor Books, 1958.

Henderson, Harold G. *Haiku in English*. New York: Japan Society, 1965. (Reprinted 1967 by Charles E. Tuttle Co., without notice or credit regarding the prior edition.)

Higginson, William J., with Penny Harter. *The Haiku Handbook: How to Write, Share, and Teach Haiku*. New York: McGraw-Hill, 1985; Tokyo: Kodansha International, 1989.

Higginson, William J., ed. *Wind in the Long Grass: A Collection of Haiku*. New York: Simon & Schuster, 1991.

Higginson, William J. *The Democracy of Haiku in North America*. The Starlight Papers 1:1. Santa Fe: From Here Press, 1993.

Higginson, William J. *Haiku Compass: Directions in the Poetical Map of the United States of America*. Tokyo: Haiku International

Association, 1994. (Bilingual English-Japanese.)

Higginson, William J., ed. *Haiku World: An International Poetry Almanac*. Tokyo: Kodansha International, in press.

Hirschfield, Jane. *The Natural World as a Carrier of Meaning in Poetry*. The Starlight Papers 1:3. Santa Fe: From Here Press, in press.

Hirshfield, Jane and Mariko Aratani, trans. *The Ink Dark Moon: Love Poems by Ono no Komachi and Izumi Shikibu, Women of the Ancient Court of Japan*. New York: Vintage Books, 1990.

Hoffman, Yoel, ed. and trans. *Japanese Death Poems: Written by Zen Monks and Haiku Poets on the Verge of Death*. Rutland Vermont and Tokyo: Charles E. Tuttle Co., 1986.

Katō, Kōko, ed. and trans. *Haiku in English from 'Sasa'*. Nagoya: Tokai Haiku Konwakai, 1985.

Keene, Donald. *World Within Walls: Japanese Literature of the Pre-Modern Era, 1600–1867*. London: Secker & Warburg, 1976.

Keene, Donald. *Some Japanese Portraits*. Tokyo: Kodansha International, 1978.

Keene, Donald. *Dawn to the West: Japanese Literature in the Modern Era: Poetry, Drama, Criticism*. New York: Henry Holt, 1984.

Kervern, Alain, ed. and trans. *Le Réveil de la Loutre: Grand Almanach Poétique Japonaise, Livre II: Le Printemps*. Romillé [Bretagne]: Éditions Folle Avoine, 1990.

Kervern, Alain, ed. and trans. *La Tisserande et le Bouvier: Grand Almanach Poétique Japonaise, Livre III: L'été*. Romillé [Bretagne]: Éditions Folle Avoine, 1992.

Kodaira, Takashi and Alfred H. Marks, trans. *The Essence of Modern Haiku: 300 Poems by Seishi Yamaguchi*. Atlanta: Mangajin, 1993.

Kondō, Shōkan, Kris Kondō, and William J. Higginson, eds. *Renku North America*. Tokyo: Association for International Renku, in preparation.

Lanoue, David G., trans. *Issa: Cup of Tea Poems, Selected Haiku of Kobayashi Issa*. Berkeley: Asian Humanities Press, 1991.

Levy, Ian Hideo, trans. *The Ten Thousand Leaves: A Translation of the* Manyōshū, *Japan's Premier Anthology of Classical Poetry.* vol. one. Princeton: Princeton U. Press, 1981.

Levy, Ian Hideo. *Hitomaro and the Birth of Japanese Lyricism.* Princeton: Princeton U. Press, 1984.

Lowitz, Leza, et al, eds. and trans. *A Long Rainy Season: Haiku & Tanka.* "Contemporary Japanese Women's Poetry, vol. 1." Berkeley: Stone Bridge Press, 1994.

Lynch, Thomas Paul. *An Original Relation to the Universe: Emersonian Poetics of Immanence and Contemporary American Haiku.* Ph.D. dissertation, University of Oregon, 1989.

McCullough, Helen Craig, trans. *Kokin Wakashū: The First Imperial Anthology of Japanese Poetry.* Stanford: Stanford U. Press, 1985.

McCullough, Helen Craig. *Brocade by Night: 'Kokin Wakashū' and the Court Style in Japanese Classical Poetry.* Stanford: Stanford U. Press, 1985.

Mesotten, Bart, ed. *Duizend Kolibries: Haikoe van Hier en Elders.* Overijse, Belgium: privately printed, 1991.

Miner, Earl, ed. and trans. *Japanese Linked Poetry: An Account with Translations of Renga and Haikai Sequences.* Princeton: Princeton U. Press, 1978.

Miner, Earl and Hiroko Odagiri, trans. *The Monkey's Straw Raincoat and Other Poetry of the Bashō School.* Princeton: Princeton U. Press, 1981.

Morris, Ivan. *The World of the Shining Prince: Court Life in Ancient Japan.* New York: Alfred A. Knopf, 1964.

Morse, Peter. *Hokusai: One Hundred Poets.* New York: George Braziller, 1989.

Murasaki Shikibu. *The Tale of Genji.* trans. Edward G. Seidensticker. 2 vols. New York: Alfred A. Knopf, 1976.

Nippon Gakujutsu Shinkōkai, trans. *The Manyōshū: One Thousand Poems.* New York: Columbia U. Press, 1965 (reprint of Tokyo: Iwanami Shoten, 1940 edn.)

Nippon Gakujutsu Shinkōkai, trans. *Haikai and Haiku*. Tokyo: Nippon Gakujutsu Shinkōkai, 1958.

Ōoka, Makoto. *The Colors of Poetry: Essays on Classic Japanese Verse*. Takako U. Lento and Thomas V. Lento, trans. Oakland, Michigan: Katydid Books, 1991.

Ōoka, Makoto. *A Poet's Anthology: The Range of Japanese Poetry*. Janine Beichman, trans. Santa Fe: Katydid Books, 1994.

Oseko, Toshiharu, ed. and trans. *Basho's Haiku / Bashō no Haiku*. Urawa, Saitama, Japan: privately printed, 1990.

Pound, Ezra. *ABC of Reading*. New York: New Directions, 1960 (reprinted from 1934).

Sakanishi, Hachirō, ed., with Shōzō Miyawaki and Horst Hammitzsch. *Issa: Übersetzung mit Kommentar und Nachdichtung Deutscher Dichter und Japanischen Scherenschnitten*. Nagano, Japan: Shinano Mainichi Shinbun, 1981.

Sakuma, Jin-ichi, ed. *Season Words in English Haiku*. San Francisco: Yuki Teikei Haiku Society of the U.S.A. and Canada, 1980.

Sato, Hiroaki. *One Hundred Frogs: From Renga to Haiku to English*. New York: Weatherhill, 1983. (Not the later, abridged edition.)

Sato, Hiroaki, trans. *Right under the big sky, I don't wear a hat: The Haiku and Prose of Hōsai Ozaki*. Berkeley: Stone Bridge Press, 1993.

Sato, Hiroaki, trans. *String of Beads: Complete Poems of Princess Shikishi*. Honolulu: U. of Hawaii Press, 1993.

Sawa, Yuki and Edith Marcombe Shiffert, eds. and trans. *Haiku Master Buson*. Union City, California: Heian International, 1978.

Shirane, Haruo. *The Bridge of Dreams: A Poetics of 'The Tale of Genji'*. Stanford: Stanford U. Press, 1987.

Shirane, Haruo. *"Aisatsu: The Poet as Guest"*, in *New Leaves: Studies and Translations of Japanese Literature in Honor of Edward Seidensticker*. Aileen Gatten and Anthony Hood

Chambers, eds. Ann Arbor, Michigan: Center for Japanese Studies, 1993.

Sommerkamp, Sabine. *Der Einfluss des Haiku auf Imagismus und Jüngere Moderne: Studien zur englishchen und amerikanischen Lyrik.* Ph.D. dissertation, University of Hamburg, 1984.

Stevens, John. trans. *Mountain Tasting: Zen Haiku by Santōka Taneda.* New York: Weatherhill, 1980.

Stryk, Lucien. *Encounter with Zen: Writings on Poetry and Zen.* Athens, Ohio: Swallow Press, 1981.

Stryk, Lucien, trans. *The Dumpling Field: Haiku of Issa.* "with the assistance of Noboru Fujiwara." Athens, Ohio: Swallow Press, 1991.

Swede, George. *The World of North American Haiku in the Year 2058.* The Starlight Papers 2:2. Santa Fe: From Here Press, in press.

Takada, Sakuzō, trans. *Excellent Haiku of Japan in the Edo Period / Nihon no Shūku: Edo Jidai Haikushū.* Selection by Nakimaro Hirose. Tokyo: Toranomon Kukai, 1991. (Bilingual Japanese-English.)

Uchida, Sono. *Haïku: Le Poème le Plus Court du Monde.* Rabat, Morocco: Éditions Techniques Nord-Africaines, 1983.

Ueda, Makoto. *Literary and Art Theories in Japan.* Cleveland: Press of Western Reserve U., 1967.

Ueda, Makoto. *Matsuo Bashō.* New York: Twayne, 1970; Tokyo: Kodansha International, 1982.

Ueda, Makoto, ed. and trans. *Modern Japanese Haiku: An Anthology.* Toronto: U. Toronto Press, 1976.

Ueda, Makoto. *Modern Japanese Poets and the Nature of Literature.* Stanford: Stanford U. Press, 1983.

Ueda, Makoto, ed. and trans. *Bashō and His Interpreters: Selected Hokku with Commentary.* Stanford: Stanford U. Press, 1991.

van den Heuvel, Cor, ed. *The Haiku Anthology: English Language Haiku by Contemporary American and Canadian Poets.* Garden City: Anchor Books, 1974.

van den Heuvel, Cor, ed. *The Haiku Anthology: Haiku and Senryu in English*. New York: Simon & Schuster, 1986. (Revised edition of above.)

Watson, Burton, trans. *Saigyō: Poems of a Mountain Home*. New York: Columbia U. Press, 1991.

Yasuda, Kenneth. *The Japanese Haiku: Its Essential Nature, History, and Possibilities in English, with Selected Examples*. Rutland, Vermont and Tokyo: Charles E. Tuttle Co., 1957.

Note: More anthologies are listed in the Acknowledgements which follow. For additional materials on haiku and related poetry in general, see the Resources section of *The Haiku Handbook*.

ACKNOWLEDGEMENTS

Many of the poems in this book by contemporary authors were sent to me in response to a call for poems issued connection with this book and its companion volume, *Haiku World: An International Poetry Almanac*, and I am very grateful to the authors for their assistance. In addition, I am grateful to the authors and publishers of the following periodicals and books for permission to include previously published work in *The Haiku Seasons*.

Periodicals (by title): *Blithe Spirit* (British Haiku Society); *Frogpond* (Haiku Society of America); *Heisei Joryū Haijin* (Mainichi Graphic); *HI* (Haiku International Association); *Modern Haiku* (Milwaukee, Wisconsin).

Books (by author or editor): Blanche, Patrick, *Rien de spécial*, Privately printed, 1992. Brooks, Randy M., and Lee Gurga, eds, *Midwest Haiku Anthology*, High/Coo Press, 1992. Cekolj, Marijan, ed, *Haiku iz Rata (Haiku from the War)*, Croation Haiku Association, 1992. Harr, Lorraine E, *The Red Barn: Variations on a Pastoral Theme in Haiku*, J & C Transcripts, 1975. Hotham, Gary, *As Far as the Light Goes*, Juniper Press, 1990. Klinge, Günther, *Day into Night: A Haiku Journey*, Charles E, Tuttle, 1980 (retranslated by WJH). Mitsuhashi, Takajo, *Mitsuhashi Takajo*, vol. 11 in Gendai Haiku no Sekai, Asahi Shinbunsha, 1984. Olson, Marian, *Songs of the Chicken Yard*, Privately printed, 1992. Ross, Bruce, ed, *Haiku Moment*, Charles E, Tuttle, 1993. Takaha, Shugyō, *One Year of Haiku*, Privately printed, |1989|. Uchida, Sonō, ed, *Haiku International 1992*, Haiku International Association, 1992. Yoshimura, Ikuyo, *At The Riverside*, Kō-no-kai, 1990.

SEASON WORD INDEX

This index includes the season words or nonseasonal keywords of all poems and stanzas in *The Haiku Seasons*. Entries in capital letters indicate a topic entry in the sample saijiki entries of Chapter 6.

GENERAL INDEX